Steadfast

A Study of the Prayer that Made David's
Whole Heart Rely on a Steadfast God

LAUREN MITCHELL

WESTBOW
PRESS®
A DIVISION OF THOMAS NELSON
& ZONDERVAN

Copyright © 2015 Lauren Mitchell.

All rights reserved. No part of this book may be used or reproduced by any means, graphic, electronic, or mechanical, including photocopying, recording, taping or by any information storage retrieval system without the written permission of the author except in the case of brief quotations embodied in critical articles and reviews.

Unless otherwise marked, scripture quotations were taken from the ESV. English Standard Version, copyright 2001 by Crossway Bibles a division of Good News Publishers.

Scripture quotations marked *Message* were taken from *The Message*. Copyright1993, 1994, 1995, 1996, 2000, 2001, 2002.

Scripture quotations marked NEB were taken from the New English Bible. Copyright 1961, 1970 by the delegates of the Oxford University Press and the syndics of the Cambridge University Press.

All word studies were taken from Biblehub.com Copyright 2004-2013 by biblios.com.

WestBow Press books may be ordered through booksellers or by contacting:

WestBow Press
A Division of Thomas Nelson & Zondervan
1663 Liberty Drive
Bloomington, IN 47403
www.westbowpress.com
1 (866) 928-1240

Because of the dynamic nature of the Internet, any web addresses or links contained in this book may have changed since publication and may no longer be valid. The views expressed in this work are solely those of the author and do not necessarily reflect the views of the publisher, and the publisher hereby disclaims any responsibility for them.

Any people depicted in stock imagery provided by Thinkstock are models, and such images are being used for illustrative purposes only. Certain stock imagery © Thinkstock.

ISBN: 978-1-4908-9577-2 (sc)
ISBN: 978-1-4908-9579-6 (hc)
ISBN: 978-1-4908-9578-9 (e)

Print information available on the last page.

WestBow Press rev. date: 10/02/15

For my own warriors of prayer who weekly seek to have a heart like God's own. My study girls...I love you.

Contents

Foreword ix

Week 1 Time
Introduction to Week 1 3

Week 2 Praise
Introduction to Week 2 23

Week 3 Identity
Introduction to Week 3 41

Week 4 Sin
Introduction to Week 4 59

Week 5 No Fear
Introduction to Week 5 79

Week 6 Destiny
Introduction to Week 6 97

Afterward and Challenge 114
Study Guide Answers 127
Notes 128
Biography 130
Acknowledgements 131

Foreword

The word Steadfast has been defined as something unwavering, firm in purpose. It is something constant, unshakeable, and changeless. The only thing I have found that comes close to meeting any of these criteria is my God.

Everything changes. There is evidence in all of nature around us. To everything there is a season. Even our lives are patterned this way. We age in seasons, we love in seasons, we bear fruit in seasons, and it never stops until we die. My favorite attribute of God in this season of my life has become Steadfast. He alone is steadfast. He alone is fixed, immovable, and constant. If you don't know Him, this sounds frightening and harsh rather than comforting and encouraging, but immovable and constant are comforting when everything else is spinning and out of control. We try to control life to feel safe. What we need is something steadfast that makes *us* immovable when everything is spinning. Change comes to everything but God: He alone is unchanging.

This is a study of the heart of David and how it was anchored in prayer. There were many seasons in David's life, seasons of sin and seasons of victory, through them all he remained a man after God's own heart. He was immovable. David became steadfast as he anchored himself to the One who is steadfast, who never changes. This enabled him to serve God with a whole and undivided heart because he was not tossed by the wind and waves of the world. David had a heart after God's own because he understood prayer. Prayer anchored the warrior poet and kept him in close communion with Steadfast love. David's whole heart relied on a steadfast God. What we hold fast to will define us. David knew his God would never change and with Him there is "no variation or shadow due to change" (James 1:17). "Jesus Christ is the same yesterday, today, and forever" (Hebrews 13:8). Amen and Amen!!!!!

In this study we are going to learn how to anchor our hearts to God's through prayer. We will look at six areas of David's life and prayer's role in each: Time, Praise, Identity, Fear, Sin, and Destiny.

Instructions:

This study isn't necessarily about brand new truths or philosophies. They may be new to you or they may not. The trouble for most of us is that we know much, but we don't put into practice what we know. We are going to take what we learn from David and the Psalms and apply it daily. This is about being accountable for all our hours and bringing Jesus into them. It's about learning to renew and focus your mind through prayer. If God is our steadfast foundation then we can become steadfast in a world where things change every minute. The more anchored we are to Jesus, the less effect the tide of the world has to pull us away or rock our boat.

Instead of blanks to fill in you will incorporate these truths into your own day and your own prayer through journaling. Don't worry there are sample prayers at the end of each day. There is additional space for you to add your own prayer at the end of both morning and evening sessions, or you can keep your prayers in your own journal. If you have never journaled a prayer in your life, pattern it after mine. I patterned mine on scripture, so you can't go wrong. Writing them will make these truths that David applied to his life your own. When you take a truth and add prayer you give it power.

Last thing, I invite you to memorize this verse from Colossians. It is a reminder of how we are to pray; steadfastly, while being expectant for answers, and always with a thankful heart.

If you are doing this study with a group, there are group sessions to use for discussion at the back of this book. They begin after finishing the first week of the study.

**Continue steadfastly in prayer
being watchful in it with thanksgiving.
Colossians 4:2**

Week 1

Time

"But the highest condition of the human will, as distinct, not as separated from God, is when, not seeing God, not seeming to itself to grasp Him at all, it yet holds Him fast."

George MacDonald

Introduction to Week 1

Time and focus. It takes time to focus. Without deliberate time in focus life blurs. Instead of a life of purpose you wind up with something that looks like modern art, the kind that takes no actual shape and is left up to interpretation. That isn't what life should be, smears of color with no clear meaning or direction, but without time and focus that is what life becomes. There is a way to make time purposeful instead of simply allowing it to pass. The key is in what you choose to spend your time focusing on. That is what decides what kind of life you will have.

The Bible leaves clear instructions as to what our focus should be. Colossians 3:2 instructs us to, "Set your minds on things that are above, not on things that are on earth". How do we put that into action? What does it mean to set our minds on things above? How do we focus on something past this temporal earth? It takes time. You have to deliberately direct your thoughts over and over to the Truth. The world in which we live becomes more and more deceptive every day. Satan evolves with better tactics of distraction all the time. Our battle is to see reality for what it actually is, not the lies that Satan would have us believe. The key to achieving a focus on Truth is repetition. See the Truth is a person. The Truth is God. The way to stay focused on Him is to pray and meditate on His word. Without this effort daily, yes I said daily, we lose focus because of the onslaught of distractions and evil which also comes against us daily. Renewing our mind is not a one time deal. Taking our thoughts captive means that when they stray, we repeatedly bring them back. The only way to achieve this is communion with God and serious time in prayer. But how much did that last sentence overwhelm you?

If we are honest we all feel pressure to pray more, but that is looking at prayer the wrong way. It isn't something to add to your list, it simplifies and directs your list. You are going to feel like you don't have the time, but you do. Spending time in prayer refines the time you spend on other things. You will find that you are less distracted and less easily led to worry. After time with God, things become clearer, and less time is wasted not knowing what to do. The last verse of the book of Job states that Job died "full of days". This verse illustrates a truth that the number of days is less important than the fullness of them. To have full days we have to give the emptiness of our time to God first and let Him fill them.

Time spent with God was a key to David's life. He was able to focus on what was important and believe the Truth because the more time he spent with God the more real God became. David left a legacy that has prevailed through ages because he focused on a steadfast God. That is what we are going to do. This week we start learning to pray by focusing on and praying God's word. There is no other way to have a steadfast life in a world where change happens every moment. If our lives are to count for eternity, we have to start focusing on eternity and realizing that this life is temporal. We have to refocus away from earth to the things above. It will take work, but everything does. It is work worth the effort. This time and focus will change not only your days on earth, but your eternity. If that isn't multitasking I don't know what is.

Morning   Day 1

This morning read Psalm 5. Now, look more closely at verse 3, "O Lord, in the morning you hear my voice; in the morning I prepare a sacrifice for you and watch". I love how *The Message* phrases it, "Every morning you'll hear me at it again. Every morning I lay out the pieces of my life on your altar and watch for fire to descend".

Did you catch the importance of the time to do this? I would go so far as to say that God understands the sacrifice of doing this in the morning, but it's the time that counts double because the day is fresh. It's a new start. God is just waiting for you to say, "Here are the puzzle pieces, I don't know where they fit, but I am going to commit them to You in prayer and be watchful for what you do. That means you expect good to come from it; that when the pieces all fit together it will be beautiful because you trust God to make it good.

Being watchful for God requires that you are reminding yourself all day. When you think about God thank Him that He is in charge. When little stresses pop up, immediately say, "Here you go God, another puzzle piece."

God I praise You that through the abundance of Your steadfast love I can enter Your house. Make Your way straight before me as I listen for You. Cover me with favor as with a shield.

Now it's your turn, take Psalm 5 and pray for your day. Be specific. Pray the scripture, and lay out your day and your thoughts for God to take and create something out of.

*Don't forget we are doing this again tonight. Keep your journal or Bible handy, or go ahead and put them on or beside your bed...or better yet on top of your pillow!

Evening

Read Psalm 16. This psalm says, "I have set the Lord always before me". Think what it means to set the Lord always before you. He is directly in your line of vision at all times. It is hard to forget or lose your purpose if it is always before you.

O God, let my eyes be set on You. Let me see only you before me and let it change how I go about my life, my hours and my days. You are my portion. You hold my lot. You are the one to look to. When my eyes stray to the earth fix my gaze back on heaven. You make known to me the path of life, there is nowhere else worth looking.

Your turn

Morning   Day 2

David was given a gift of aloneness. He was a shepherd; you don't get much more removed from people than that. I don't know many sheep, but they have never struck me as great conversationalists. Because of his aloneness, David would have had quality time to talk to God. God used this time to prepare his heart. Even after being anointed King, David spent countless hours hidden away in caves, facing fear and being on the run… alone. Alone….

There are 73 psalms attributed to the authorship of David. If he had this many prayers not just written down but recorded to be read or sung publicly, imagine how many he could have simply penned as a shepherd alone under the stars. He would have had nothing but time to sit in awe of God's glory and respond to it. Time can give you the opportunity to make a list of doubts or a list of assurances. David used his to make assurances. He strengthened his faith by setting his heart on what was true, just as Moses "endured as seeing Him who is invisible" (Hebrews 11:27). David made the invisible seem more visible. Not just for himself, but for those men who where watching him, the ones that flocked to him. They saw his struggle and they saw what he did with it. He set his heart on God. The more you focus on something and talk about it and think on it, the more real it becomes.

"Faith is like radar that sees through the fog - the reality of things at a distance that the human eye cannot see." Corrie ten Boom

Now read psalm 65. We are going to make the going out of the morning and the evening shout for joy, or rather I should say we are going to join them morning and evening for the next six weeks. When you pray, ask Him for the time. He will provide it. When you put God first, everything else falls into place. You will have all the time you need. You are actually gaining time. Your time will count. It will make a difference in eternity and your day!

God all praise is due to you! Thank you that You are a God who hears our prayer. I want to be one You choose to bring near, to dwell in your courts even while I am here on earth. Thank you that You satisfy like nothing else. You make the going out of the morning and the evening to shout for joy. Thank you for mornings where there is the promise of a fresh start and evenings, the promise of rest. Thank you that You set up our lives in these divisions because you knew we needed them. Give me discernment for how to use my gift of hours. Let me give my time to You and watch You multiply it like the five loaves and two fishes.

Your turn

Evening

Tonight read Psalm 37. I researched the word fret from this text. It is the Hebrew "charah" which means "to be kindled". When we fret we are kindling a fire. It may be a fire of anxiety or anger, but we are kindling and nursing that fire just the same. This morning I talked about David making a list of assurances rather than a list of doubts. He used prayer to put out fires in his mind before they got out of control and took over his actions.

Thank you that I can trust you. I need not fret. Thank you that Your word helps me put out that fire by affirming that when I trust You and commit my way to You; You will act. I can be still and wait for You, I don't have to strive and battle myself. Exodus 14:14 says, "The Lord will fight for you; you need only be still." You uphold the righteous. You know my days and my heritage will remain forever. Establish my steps and thank you that if I fall You hold my hand. Teach me to turn away from evil and do good.

Your turn...make it personal to you.

Morning   Day 3

There is an old movie I have always loved called "Somewhere in Time". It's a love story starring Christopher Reeves and Jane Seymour. Reeves is a playwright and at one of his opening nights an old woman comes up to him and presses a watch in his hands and says, "Come back to me." He becomes curious and finally tracks her down. He finds that she died the night she visited him. Her caretaker explains that she was a famous actress in her day until she met a man and fell in love, but the man mysteriously disappeared. After that, she never acted again. Reeves becomes obsessed with her. He starts finding out all he can about time travel and eventually makes it back in time and falls in love with her. To travel back, he must totally convince himself that the past is his reality. Everything around him and on him must teach his brain that it really is 1923. That is exactly what we must do, except we must convince ourselves that our future is our reality. If we can submerse ourselves in God, His presence, His word, then He is our reality and the promises He made become fact. I am not trying to tell you its something magical; it's the way the brain works. The more you focus on something the more real it becomes.

We are to run the race fixed on the prize (1 Corinthians 9:24). We are to lay down this life in exchange for something much better. Sports analogies are not any different. It works. Where your heart is, there also your treasure will be. Except I am saying that where your heart is, is in fact where you focus. Just like anything else worth having, focus takes self-control. Self-control always sounded like a self-help gimmick to me, until I was taught that it is a fruit of the spirit. It doesn't matter how much determination I have on my own without the Holy Spirit in me, I am doomed. You have probably heard someone in your life tell you that people don't change. Without the Holy Spirit, they don't. With the Holy Spirit, I am capable of as much as God wants to accomplish in my life. But as I stated before it isn't magic; it's focus. "Faith is the gaze of a soul upon a saving God." A.W. Tozer. The more fixed our gaze the stronger our faith.

How much God do you want? Seriously, this is not a rhetorical question. Answer it, in your heart or in your journal I don't care, but answer the question. Do you want a zeal for God that consumes you? Yes, I said consumes you, as in devours you, overshadows you and what you want. Do you want to make the invisible so visible to you that others even start to see Him? Because it costs; it costs time and beyond that it will cost you other things too. What it will cost each of us differs, but it will. I write this with conviction mingled with fear in my own heart. I know I said "you" for effect, but I mean us. If we want the invisible God to be seen in our lives, then we have to stop seeing us. To get us out of the way we have to see more of Him. How does He become more visible to you, how does He become your reality? Focus….Time…

Now read Psalm 108 and hear David's heart. "My heart is steadfast, O God!" the KJV says, "My heart is fixed" (v.1). I cry with David, my heart is steadfast!

Father fix my heart. I don't want to fall short of the mark. I want my heart to be steadfast. I want others to see You because You can be seen in me. I want to be so sure of my God that others can visibly see you. You are reality. Satan works so hard to blind us to what is real and what is true. Open our eyes. Grant us help against our foe. With You God, we shall do valiantly, without You we are lost. Remind us that our efforts are nothing but vanity. At the same time strengthen us to go valiantly where You lead us.

Your turn

Evening

Tonight I want you to read Psalm 108 in the *Message* translation if you have access to it. I love how it says, I'm ready God, from head to toe. In the other two translations we examined how David says, I'm steadfast; I'm fixed. We can't be ready to be used by God until we are fixed on Him.

All that time David spent as a shepherd, in caves, alone…It wasn't waiting, it was changing. God had to change his reality before he could be the man God needed. He couldn't be King until he really learned that he wasn't. He was just a shepherd. He had to learn how much he needed God. He had to learn how God kept him. He had to learn how God answers prayer. He had to learn that it is God who gives strength and power. He had to learn obedience. He had to learn how praise stills fear, and countless other things, some of which we are going to talk about and some we may never know.

Fortunately, God will ask very few of us to go to the extreme of living on the run in a cave, but thankfully He also isn't going to ask us to be a King over His people, but He will ask each of us to do something. We can't accomplish eternal goals if we aren't fixed on eternity. Eternity has to become our reality. "For to set the mind on the flesh is death, but to set the mind on the spirit is life and peace" (Romans 8:6).

Your turn

Morning   Day 4

This morning read Psalm 86. In verse 11 David says, "Teach me your way, O Lord, that I may walk in your truth; unite my heart to fear your name." Unite my heart. What would it take to have an undivided, whole heart? What pulls at yours? Sometimes we let things get in the way of our heart's purpose. Our heart becomes divided. They aren't bad things in themselves; they become bad only when we elevate them to a place in our hearts they shouldn't be. Look at how you spend your time, it will show you where your heart lies. It's funny how little it takes to distract us. A distracted heart isn't whole, it isn't united. The book of Jeremiah agrees, "You will seek me and find me when you seek me with all your heart" (Jeremiah 29:13).

"Draw near to God; he will draw near to you. Cleanse your hands, you sinners, and purify your hearts, you double-minded." (James 4:8). Did you note the second part of that verse? I usually only ever hear the first part quoted! The first part is a wonderful promise so I am not trying to overshadow that, but look at the other half of the instructions. We are to purify our hearts because we are double-minded! Double minded!!!! The NLT states that phrase like this, "Purify your hearts for your loyalty is divided between God and the world". Wow!!!! That word double-minded is the Greek word dipsuchos (dip'-soo-khos) meaning, "double minded, wavering (lit: of two souls, of two selves)." It goes on to describe a person split in half. Ever felt split in half? God totally knew we would feel this way; He knew we would feel double-minded and we would waiver. He tells us here that we don't have to. The reason we need God and long for Him so much is that He is steadfast! He doesn't waiver! Draw near to Him and feel his stability. That is the only way to purify our hearts of the world. If we are divided, we aren't effective.

It takes time to reset your mind on eternal things and away from earthly things. The Grand Canyon wasn't carved in a day. It is hard work to focus our thoughts. It isn't a one time thing. It's an everyday, every hour thing. It takes an investment in time. Old habits die hard, but they need to be put to death. God is not going to use our half-heartedness; He wants our whole hearts.

Let me cry to you all the day, especially when my heart gets divided Lord. Thank you that You abound in steadfast love to those who call on You. There is none like You, You alone are God. Teach me Your way that I may walk in Your truth with unwavering steps. Unite my heart to fear Your name only and drown out the call of the world that splits me in two.

Your turn

Evening

We already talked about James 1:5-8. Read that again to refresh your memory. Catch any familiar words? James used that same phrase ""double-minded that we read this morning. A double-minded man is unstable in all his ways, tossed like a wave of the sea. James is talking about asking for wisdom from God and that we should ask in faith with no doubting. That may seem off topic a little, so let me explain. I propose to you that we can purify our hearts from being double minded by drawing near to the one who is steadfast. Only He can unite your heart and make you whole, only He can make you stable in all your ways, only He can take your divided heart and make it only His. Then when you ask Him for the wisdom you need, He can trust you with it. He can know it will be spent on His purposes because your whole heart is focused on Him. He can give you wisdom about who to talk to, how your time is best spent, and what you do with your life without fighting the distraction and pull of the world at the same time. God can teach us His way and we can walk in truth when He unites our hearts to fear only His name. God is not going to use our half-heartedness. He wants our whole hearts.
If you want to remain steadfast and not be tossed and driven by the wind, there is no other way than to hold fast to something that is immovable. Holding fast is not something you can do casually. You either commit to keep a tight grip or you are washed away. There is no middle ground. We all act like there is, but in truth you are either holding fast and staying closely anchored to God, or the tide of the world is in control of your life and emotions. So the question is how to hold fast. The answer is time and focus.

Read 1 Chronicles 28:9-10. This was David's charge to his son. Did you notice the words "whole heart"? He knew that many things would try and divide his son's heart. He knew that the double-minded would be unstable. David knew that his son would need to be steadfast and the only way to be steadfast was to cling to the Rock. He told Solomon what could be his downfall. Unfortunately Solomon let his heart be divided by many things.

Now for tonight read Psalm 139.

God you know me, you discern my thoughts! Where can I go? Let this thought be a comfort to me. The fact that "You hem me it behind and before, and you lay your hand upon me", makes me think of a baby swaddled tightly. You know I can't handle much wiggle room or I will start to think I have some control and never settle and rest. Let the pressure of Your hand give me peace. Keep me close to You, pull my thoughts back to You, then every moment counts. When I get consumed by the things of the world and darkness steels in, even dark isn't dark to You and all I have to do is say Your name to bring my thoughts back to Your thoughts, make Your thoughts precious to me. Search me and know my thoughts. Correct what is dividing my heart and lead me in the way everlasting!

Your turn

Morning   Day 5

This morning read Psalm 62. "For God alone my soul waits in silence" (v. 1). This is a stretch for me. (Okay I heard your laughter). Seriously, I am rarely silent, even when I am alone. Sit and be silent with God and listen. Read that psalm again.

"He alone is my rock and my salvation, my fortress; I shall not be greatly shaken" (v.2). The KJV says "moved" instead of "shaken". You cannot be steadfast if nothing ever tries to move you. Likewise you cannot understand God as the anchor of your soul until you cling to what doesn't move, until you also don't move. David could only become steadfast by learning to cling to God, as close as he could get. Then he could hold fast to the hope set before him because he had God as the sure and steadfast anchor of his soul (Hebrews 6:19). I think being steadfast has to do with our frequency of contact with God. The more you try Him, the more you need Him, the more you need Him, the more He gives, the more of God you get, the more immovable you will become. Then, when the waves toss and the wind blows, we don't move, not because of us, but because of our anchor.

Let me put it another way. What we rehearse becomes automatic. That's why there are rehearsals. When the time comes and you get stage fright, whatever lines were rehearsed will come out because they were practiced. In our lives, when the distractions, lies, fear, etc. come, whatever we have rehearsed will be our reaction. My piano teacher, I can't even remember the woman's name, she used to say "practice makes permanent." She was right.

Father, I desire to be steadfast as much as that scares me. I confess I don't really want the waves, but I do want to feel Your steadiness. Help me cling to You as closely as I can. I want an anchored soul that is not tossed by the world because it understands the strength of the One who holds it. God make me less easily shaken because my treasure is not on this earth. My real treasure cannot be touched by time and will never be shaken.

Your turn

Evening

This evening I want you to look back and think about the things we have said. Meditate on the truth of anything you journaled and the scriptures we have read. We are going to practice being watchful in it with thanksgiving (Colossians 4:2). You can't be watchful for an answer if you don't remember what you prayed for, that is one of the great things about having prayers written down! Answered prayer is to be taken notice of. It increases faith. It can change our reactions and rude assumptions. We need to practice our reactions to what God does, big and little, under the assumption that it is good. For that to be our default we have to undo the thinking of the world. The way to do that is to pray concrete truths and watch God happen. He loves to show off, particularly when His children are watching in hope, and being thankful.

Now for tonight, read Psalm 34. I am just going to tell you that if you don't have to read that twice there is something wrong! Notice in verse 8 David says, "Taste and see that the Lord is good!" This is the reverse order of what the world says. You don't taste it until you see that it is good. With God we are to know it's good before we taste, we are to trust. We taste and then we see the good.

God I will bless you at all times. Remind me to do this all day tomorrow. Your praise shall continually be in my mouth! Let others notice my praise of You tomorrow that they be compelled to praise you also.. Let my soul only boast in You. Thank you that when we seek You we lack no good thing. When our afflictions are many You deliver us! Help us watch for You to do it! Give us eyes to see.

Your turn

Week 2

Praise

(The "But God" Principle)

"Through prayer, God has given to everyone the right to take hold of Him and His strength."

Andrew Murray

Introduction to Week 2

Praise

This world is fraught with trouble, each day brings it's own. Instead of fighting against the waves of this world, we are called to hold fast to a steadfast God. No matter what waves may come, and they will come, we can't take our focus off God to fight them in our strength. If we are holding God with both hands and He isn't moving, neither are we. We waiver when we think to fight against our circumstances instead of letting them work their purpose, causing us to cling tighter to our Redeemer. When we let go with even one hand to fight those waves our stability is more easily shaken. You cannot be steadfast if nothing ever tries to move you.

This week we are going to study a phrase that appears in scripture 3,930 times. David used it over and over in the psalms. Every Psalm is an illustration of David's vulnerablitily versus God's strength, and God's strength wins every time. The phrase is "But God". It occurs in multiple bible stories when the chips are down and humans are out of luck. At that moment when hope is lost there is a "But God". It's the theme for our entire history with God. Salvation itself rests on this phrase. When humanity could never be enough there was a "But God".

> **"But God being rich in mercy, because of the great Love with which He loved us, even when we were dead in our trespasses, made us alive together with Christ -by grace you have been saved-"**
> **Ephesians 2:4&5**

Morning   Day 1

David did not fear emotion. He was a mighty man who feared neither giants, armies, nor Kings. Just as impressive to me, he had no fear of his feelings. Now women, we know about feelings. Men, however, are not as acquainted with their feelings. There are few men who do not fear feelings…their own or other people's!!! I think men don't always understand feelings. They are afraid of what they might mean, or of appearing weak. Of all the characteristics that David brings to mind, weak is not one of them. He knew that his feelings were safe with God. Did you catch that? They were safe with God away from prying eyes that might judge him as weak, enabling him to be a man that inspired fearlessness. Men were created to be *Men*. They are the protectors and the providers. Their presence is supposed to inspire confidence and feelings of safety. David inspired that! Men flocked to him. They flocked to him because of his strength. He became steadfast and strong and not pulled by emotions because his God is steadfast and strong. David could lead because he knew who to follow. Men will not follow you if you are not steadfast but moved by every feeling and emotion. I am not saying that David didn't have them, he was a poet, but instead of spilling his emotions everywhere, he took them to God.

We talked last week about having a double-mind or a divided heart. That is exactly what emotions and feelings can do to us. This week we are going to practice a pattern of prayer that stills the enemy when he tries to use our emotions against us. I call it the" But God principle" I want you to read the following Psalm 3 and circle the "But" when it appears.

Did you see it? The first two verses talk of the many rising against him and then there is a "But". "But you, O Lord are a shield about me, my glory, and the lifter of my head." (Psalm 3:3). I want you to be on the lookout for these this week. They may appear in different forms of words, but you will recognize the shift in mindset of the psalm. It signifies a turning point when David took his emotions to God and the prayer changed his mood and mind. He sets up every problem and then follows it with the Lord as the solution. Did you catch that? He doesn't come up with a solution or what God is going to do, the Lord *is* the solution. My favorite verse in the book of Romans is 8:24, "Wretched man that I am, Who will deliver me from this body of death?" The next verse answers the question: Jesus! I don't need the list of steps to the solution, Jesus is the solution. He is the Who! David got that. To every problem the solution is But God!

David talks in Psalm 3 of his foes and he asks God to strike his enemy on the cheek (v.3).
David was a man of battle, and I love that about him. He used prayer to go on the offense against his foe. Who is our foe? We are to wage spiritual war on Satan. He assaults our thoughts all the time and our defensive weapon is the shield of faith. We put up our faith in God by affirming it in prayer and out loud. We have an offensive weapon too, the sword, which is the word of God (Ephesians 6). When we use it in prayer it is a double whammy!

Read Psalm 3 again. Now ask God to be the lifter of your head and to identify what Satan is rising against you. Then you write down your "But God"!

Thank you God that when my many thoughts are rising up against me, You are my shield and the lifter of my head. Thank you that when You lift my head I can meet your gaze and it focuses me by reminding me of who You are. Make me strong for battle and use me to defeat my enemy today.

Your turn

Evening

We have already read Psalm 86, but I want you to read it again. This time circle the "But".

In verse 11 David asks God, "Teach me your way". That word translated "teach" is actually the Hebrew word "yarah" (Yaw-raw) which means, "to throw or shoot as an arrow, to point or teach". David is saying, God, use me as your arrow; use me to point to you. This week we go to battle, and we ask God to use us as his arrow. We can be used to thwart Satan's battle plan. WE can be used as God's arrow every time we meditate and speak Truth. We can be an arrow that strikes Satan and sets him running.

O God, to You do I lift up my soul. You are quick to meet my gaze and remind me of truth. Use me as Your arrow. Make me fly straight and swift right to the heart of Satan. Be gracious to me, I cry to You all the day because I need you all the day. But You, O Lord, are abounding in steadfast love and faithfulness.

Your turn…

Morning   Day 2

Read Psalm 103. This time I want you to circle the "But" and "steadfast love". Remember Romans 8:24, God is the "Who" we need!
David Martyn Lloyd Jones asks, "Have you realized that most of your unhappiness in life is due to the fact that you are listening to yourself instead of talking to yourself ?". We have to learn to talk to ourselves, to remind ourselves of our blessings and our future. When we listen to ourselves it focuses us on who *we* are and our failures. When we talk to ourselves we focus on who *He* is and His faithfulness.

1 Bless the Lord, O my soul,
and all that is within me,
bless his holy name!
2 Bless the Lord, O my soul,
and forget not all his benefits,
3 who forgives all your iniquity,
who heals all your diseases,
4 who redeems your life from the pit,
who crowns you with steadfast love and mercy,
5 who satisfies you with good
so that your youth is renewed like the eagle's.

Now I want you to bless the Lord and list all the benefits you can think of. Writing them helps us not forget them.

I mean it…write them in your journal.

O God time would fail me to tell of all Your benefits! I am so thankful that you do not deal with us according to our sins! You are slow to anger abounding in steadfast love. You redeem my life from the pit. Your steadfast love is from everlasting to everlasting and Your righteousness to my children's children.

Your turn

Evening

Read Psalm 145 out loud. Yes for real. Then pen your prayer and sleep knowing that "the Lord is near to all who call on Him, to all who call on him in truth" (v.14).

Father let me call on You in truth with full assurance that my prayers are heard. Teach me truth about myself. When I feel out of control remind me to meditate on Your works day and night. Make me faithful to tell of your works to the next generation.

Your turn

Morning   Day 3

Before you read this morning, take a moment and bless the Lord by recalling his benefits from yesterday...and if possible, do it on your knees.

Prior to reading Psalm 55 today, we need a little context. This psalm was written after David's son first launched his insurrection. That means David's own son was trying to kill and overthrow him. Hear his emotion and his pain and then circle the "But" in verse 16 and hear the tide change.

God has to be our "But" in every circumstance. I cannot imagine David dealing with these circumstances! But I am awed at how he responded to them. Did you note that he is human? He indicates that "evening, and morning, and at noon I utter my complaint and moan and he hears my voice" (v.17). He feels safe to complain, but he never leaves it at that. There is always a "But". That fact is what made him capable of battle and action. He didn't remain useless. He did not allow his pain to paralyze him. He took it to God, and he left it there. He had to repeat the process over and over...just like us.

I read a quote by Spurgeon yesterday; it is penned in my bible beside Psalm 6:6, "I am weary with my moaning; every night I flood my bed with tears..." the quote says, "Tears are liquid prayers that need no interpretation." When I have no words, He still hears. God sees; He knows. Allow Him to take the tears and make them useful. Thank Him for hearing. Thank Him that He redeems our souls from the battle that we wage (v. 18). Then go to battle, still the enemy with praise, and let God use you as his arrow.

Father thank You for knowing every tear that falls. Thank you even more that there will be a day when the last tear falls, and then no more. Keep us focused on that day and that time. Let our hours here reflect a heart set on heaven.

Teach us how praise can be an arrow that strikes Satan right in the heart. When I am restless because of the noise of the enemy help my thankfulness and praise drown out his voice. Don't let us become paralyzed by our pain. Because of Your steadfast love, do not let us be moved.

Your turn

Evening

I want you to read Psalm 69 tonight. This Psalm is the second most quoted psalm in all of the New Testament. I hate to even comment on this Psalm because it speaks for itself.
Make sure you circle the "But".

"But as for me, my prayer is to you, O Lord. At an acceptable time, O God, in the abundance of your steadfast love, answer me in your saving faithfulness" (v. 13). This verse speaks worlds about prayer that makes us steadfast. David makes his request trusting in God's steadfast love to answer in His time. Then he affirms who God is with praise of His saving faithfulness which strengthens David's own faith. Now *that* is how to pray.

Reread verses 29&30. David knew that recalling God's salvation could set him on high in the midst of pain. He purposed to praise Him with a song and to magnify Him with thanksgiving. That is what I want you to do right now. I want you to journal a request for yourself or for someone you love that is in pain. Tell God you will trust his acceptable time. Then I want you to praise God with a song. I mean it, put on your favorite praise song and belt it out! If you are doing this as a group study, you will share some of your favorite lyrics this week. So make sure you write a segment in your journal after your prayer.

But as for me, my prayer is to You, always to You. Thank You that You are never too busy for us. Thank you that You answer prayers at the right time, not a moment too late or too soon. Thank you for your steadfast love which falls down on us in abundance. You are a God of abundance, let us not forget it.

Your turn

Morning   Day 4

Get ready to be excited! I love this next part. It makes me want a slingshot and five stones!!!

Read Psalm 9. This psalm was written by David right after he slew Goliath. Did you note the "But" in verse 7? If you didn't, go back and circle it. His "But" was that the Lord is on His throne so there is nothing to fear. I want you to write verse 10 here:

Now go to 1 Samuel 17: 45-47. What did David say he came at Goliath with…the name of the Lord! Please don't misunderstand here, I am not teaching a name it and claim it theology. It is important to note the whole text. David did not do this for his glory, he did it so that "all the earth may know that there is a God in Israel" (v.46). He understood that the battle was the Lord's and that the Lord saves not with sword and spear (v. 47).

So today we are going to face our giants with the name of the Lord. Not just yours, I want you to journal a prayer in the name of the Lord for someone you love. I want you to ask specifically and with trust in His name. Then I want you to pen a prayer for yourself. Sometime today text, write a note, or even call that person you prayed for. Tell them you were praying down their Giants in the name of the Lord. When he answers the prayer, remember that the glory is always the Lord's however he chooses to answer.

"May the power of Christ be the measure of my expectations."
Andrew Murray

Father I pray that Your power would be the measure of our expectations. Let Your mercy be the reminder that You give Your best. Help us to take Your answers as the gifts we know they are. Don't let us ray cowardly prayers out of fear that You will not answer. That is not how You taught. In the same way, let us not forget who we are addressing. Keep us thankful and humble. Remind us that You are on Your throne so fear has no place in our hearts.

Your turn

Evening

Read Psalm 8. Let's look specifically at verse 2. "Out of the mouth of babies and infants, you have established strength because of your foes, to still the enemy and the avenger."

What comes from the mouths of infants that stills the enemy? Praise does. Jesus quoted this psalm to the Pharisees in Matthew 21 when he cleansed the temple. The children started crying out," Hosanna to the Son of David" (v.15). The Pharisees became angry,
"And they said to him, "Do you hear what these are saying?" And Jesus said to them, "Yes; have you never read, "'Out of the mouth of infants and nursing babies you have prepared praise'?" (v.16). God established strength in praise! When we praise we are strengthened because we are reminded of God's ability and not our lack of it. Our focus is taken from our certain failure to God's guaranteed victory.

As I write this Caleb, my youngest, sits here beside me, yogurt all over his face babbling away; and I ask are you praising Jesus....he smiles.

Father, thank you that you gave us praise. That we have a tool that lifts us because it takes our eyes off of ourselves and our limitations and helps us focus on You and Your infinite power. Thank you that today I can praise You at any time, no matter what I am doing and it will turn the moment into a holy one. When the enemy of my soul starts to work on me and remind me of myself, I can combat those thoughts with thoughts of You and he will be stopped in his tracks. Remind me of Your love in the morning that I begin my day with thoughts of You.

Your turn

Morning   Day 5

Read Psalm 59 and circle the "But".

Thank God that He is our strength and tell Him that you will watch for Him to meet you. He will. Record how He does. Sing of His strength and His steadfast love in the morning! Seriously, put on some praise and then go journal.

God I lack strength so often and it leads me to feel frustrated and exhausted. Change my reaction to this need and let me ask you for strength and then watch for you to supply it. Then teach me to praise you before I even get the answer knowing that praise changes my focus.

Your turn

Evening

Read Psalm 52 and circle the two "Buts". Most commentaries agree that David is referring to Saul in these opening verses. He lamented the kind of king that Saul had become. He knew that God would eventually break him down forever. Saul would be uprooted and David would be planted like a "green olive tree in the house of God". Re-read verses 8&9. David would wait because he knew God would do it for His namesake. He would trust in the steadfast love of God. We are going to talk more about that later. For tonight, just pen your heart to God, and tell Him what you are willing to wait and trust Him for.

God I will sing of Your strength when I feel the lack of strength in me. I will sing of Your steadfast love to start my morning. I will watch for you expecting Your strength to fill me with what I need. Thank you that my victory depends on the one in me and not on my strength.

Your turn

WEEK 3

Identity

"Men would rather receive salvation from God than God their salvation."

George MacDonald

Introduction to Week 3

Identity

Identity is a person's conception and expression of who they are. It is twofold. Who you conceive yourself to be directly relates to your expression of who you are. Often we act in a way that does not express who we really are because our conception is off. We are sons and daughters of the King. The one King, creator of the universe is our Father and we are joint heirs with Christ. That is a powerful identity.

This week we will talk about how Satan tries to attack our identity. If he can change our conception of who we are, he can ruin our expression of Christ. You see Satan doesn't really care about us. It isn't our identity he is attacking. He knows that on our own, we are no threat to him whatsoever. When he attacks our identity; he is really attacking Jesus in us. If he can get us to think that we are only who *we* are, and we can do only what *we* are capable of then we aren't dangerous at all.

Think again on what I said about Satan attacking Jesus and not us. If you think of it that way, we are far too complacent when we should be offended. He isn't attacking us; he's attacking our Redeemer, the man who gave everything to save us. We take that far too lightly. Without Christ we don't amount to a hill of beans and the things Satan can accuse us of may be true, but we aren't without Christ, Hallelujah! We are in Christ! When God looks at us He sees His perfect son. There are no accusations left because it has been finished. Jesus paid it all! So when Satan comes to attack your identity, remind him of the truth and he will quickly retreat.

Morning   Day 1

Now this is about to give you chill bumps! For the context of this psalm you need to read 2 Samuel 21:15-17. Then go ahead and read Psalm 27. This psalm was written after the battle in 2 Samuel when David was sent back to camp. The men feared that David would be killed in battle and the light of Israel would go out. So David went back to camp and wrote;

"The Lord is *my* **light** and *my* salvation;
Whom shall I fear?
The Lord is the stronghold of my life;
of whom shall I be afraid?" (v.1)

Did you notice that I made the word light **bold** and <u>underlined</u>? If I could have made it flash at you I would have! No matter how many times I read this, I can't get over it. David says you are confused men, you think I am the light when I am not. There is only one Light of Israel! Verse 14 makes me want to sing! David says, "Wait for the Lord". Don't hang your hopes on me. David knew exactly who he was and who he wasn't. It enabled him to lead and point to God at the same time. He could say your courage and strength don't come from me, they come from the Lord.

David knew the Light. David knew the One who was steadfast, and he clung to Him. That made David immovable also. Men flocked to him because of this! The amount that you will cling to Jesus is the amount of faith you will project. The tighter you hold the less you move. The less you are moved, the more men will see the difference and God will get glory!

Read verse 8 aloud as a prayer to God. When we seek his face and that is all we seek His light reflects off of us and all will see.

Father, I ask that you let my confidence rest in You. Let others see my confidence and notice it is unlike that of the world. I have no need to fear because of You, not my preparations or manipulations in an attempt to control my circumstances. Let me seek your face all the days of my life.

Your turn

Evening

This evening read Psalm 112.

"For the righteous will never be moved;
He will be remembered forever.
He is not afraid of bad news,
His heart is firm, trusting in the Lord.
His heart is steady; he will not be afraid." (Vs. 6-8)

Go back and underline the characteristics of the righteous. All of these characteristics speak of a man who clings to the Steadfast God. It is the only way to never be moved. David has definitely been remembered forever, but it is not because of him, but the Lord. Whether you are remembered by man or not, God never forgets you.

Father if I am remembered at all let it be because of Your light shining through me. Remind me when I am flattered not to take it to heart, but to submit my heart to You. Help me not to fear bad news because my heart is steady, trusting in You. Make my heart firm and bring me peace for my anxiousness.

Your turn

Morning   Day 2

Read Psalm 22 and circle the two places it states "Yet you are". David was clearly in the dark during this psalm. I believe Satan was working overtime to attack his identity and mock him. In two verses he asks to be saved from the mouth of the lion. (Psalm 22:13&21). Satan is referred to as a lion in 1 Peter 5:8, this is not coincidental. Remember how I had you circle those phrases? I think that David answered Satan's attacks with God's identity. "Yet you are holy" (Psalm 22:3), meaning I don't have a defense for myself, but You are holy. Men or Satan can accuse us all day long; it will not change our standing in Christ, even if what they say about us is true. We would do well to remember that when God looks at us; He sees Jesus. If we truly believe this in our heart, we can shut Satan down before he starts. Did you catch all of the references to Jesus in this psalm? Again I don't think that is a coincidence. David could say to Satan, what I have been or what I have done doesn't matter because God took me and now I am identified with Jesus.

David understood that God had more to do with his physical birth than even his parents, "you are He who took me from the womb….you have been my God" (v.9&10). I am not belittling the role of parents in our life, but it is God who knit us together. He deserves the glory for what we become. David understood that your identity does not rest on your earthly family.

I don't want you to think that those who have come before us play no role in who we become. Note that David could look to his fathers, the men of faith who came before and remember that "they trusted and were not put to shame" (v.5). Heritage is important. I am thankful that no matter what our earthly heritage is, we are identified with Christ and we inherit His. Satan cannot use our family against us, because our identity does not rest on them. We can reassure our faith by looking back on the same men of faith David did because we are adopted into that same lineage. We are also able to make a heritage of faith for our children, even if it starts with us. (Galatians, Hebrews, &Romans assure us of this truth).

Thank God for His identity and that we rest in it and not our own. If there are members of your own family that have left you a heritage of faith, take time to thank God for them. Maybe even write them a note thanking them if they are still this side of heaven.

David's own lineage reflected the fact that identity is not all in your genes, but more about the degree to which you seek God. David's line included some Kings who led the nation to repentance and some who plunged them into idolatry. There was one King that came from the seed of David who was like no other. His identity is what changes ours.

Father thank you that my King is like no other. Thank you for giving me a heritage like no other. Let me simple hear only what You say about me. Let that alone be where I find my identity. Let me act like the one You say I am.

Your turn

Evening

Tonight read Psalm 10 and pay special attention to verse 14. It's the "But" that changes everything. God does see. He sees the fatherless, He sees all injustice, He sees all evil, and He will remember. "He will incline His ear to do justice….and man who is of the earth may strike terror no more" (Psalm 10:17&18). This is what makes it okay for us to forgive. God takes care of the rest. If we don't forgive, we allow our identity to be defined by those who have hurt us.

Thank God tonight that He remembers all the injustice that has ever been done to you. Then ask Him to help you forget.

Father thank you that You see everything. You have not missed a moment of my life. You judge my heart rightly and give me the mercy and grace I need. I thank you that you forgive those who have hurt me just like you forgive me for the people I have hurt. When I start to feel a desire for justice, remind me that I have not received what I deserved.

Your turn

Morning   Day 3

David didn't have an identity problem. David understood that he was just a man. He knew who he was, and who he wasn't. He might be King, but he knew that was only entrusted to him as long as God decided. He had watched Saul become a man who was not fit to be king. He knew the delicate balance. Saul did have an identity problem. He was insecure. 1 Samuel 15:17 says that Saul was little in his own eyes. Saul did not understand who he was as a child of God which led him to try and make himself bigger in his own eyes. In this same chapter we see Saul put up a monument to himself. In Contrast, David spent a lifetime collecting things and making plans for the House of God, even though he wouldn't get to build it. The credit would belong to His son.

Knowing who you are in Christ is also important because it can protect you from jealousy. Because Saul found himself little in his own eyes, he became threatened by David's success. His fragile self-esteem couldn't take the blow. When Saul's ears heard these songs being sung, 'Saul has struck down his thousands, and David his ten thousands'" (1 Samuel 18:7), he became enraged. Talk about a blow to the ego, and Saul was too fragile to handle it. Saul only served God half-heartedly because he was divided between God and his own glory. David allowed God to make his heart whole by constant dependence. David knew he was not steadfast, only God was. If David was to remain steadfast, he had to remain in God.

Read Psalm 18. I hope you noted how much He, God, did. David knew that it was God who lit his lamp, only God could make him run against a troop, and advance against a wall (vs.28&29).

Journal a prayer and make sure you make a list of the things He can do through you so that you are reminded of Who God is and as a result, who we are.

God let us never forget Who You are, and in the same way let us not forget who we are because of You. When we begin to feel little remind us that we are, but we serve a God that is not. We are joint heirs with Christ (Romans 8:17).

We have an inheritance with Him. Remind us of our importance to You and let that be our identity. Purge us of our self-importance and make our hearts whole so that they can be used by You.

Your turn

Evening

Read Psalm 12 and take note of verse 2. "Everyone utters lies to his neighbor; with flattering lips and a double heart they speak". Double hearts don't speak the truth because they are divided in their agenda. Flattering lips have the purpose of making the person addressed feel important, and the person speaking feel they have forged a loyalty from the hearer. But because flattery implies it is not true, it cannot be trusted. Man cannot be trusted period. Only God can judge the intentions of the heart. As King, men would have flattered David left and right to try and forge an allegiance. David had an identity founded in Christ which reminded him he was nothing and Christ was everything or he would not have had a whole heart. It would be a great practice, at least for me, to ask God to help us instantly forget when someone flatters us so that it does not lodge in our hearts. Only God can keep our hearts whole. We would be wise to pray verse 7 daily.

God Guard me from this generation forever. Only Your thoughts are pure like silver refined seven times. Let Your thoughts about me become mine so that I feel safe in my identity as Your dearly loved children and heir with Christ, and don't feel a need to make my own name great.

Your turn

Morning   Day 4

This morning read Psalm 17. Now read verses1-5 again. I used to think that David was really brazen to say these kinds of things. But I get it now. David could say that his steps had held fast and his feet had not slipped because God had visited him and tried his heart. If you are in close contact with God all day and night, then you don't have outstanding sins cluttering up your communication. If you have asked God to test your heart TODAY, then you can say these things with assurance. The frequency of David's communication allowed for no time to forget. He didn't forget that he was forgiven nor did he forget the One who forgave. His identity was reassured by close and frequent contact with the One who defined him.

We are going to re-read Psalm 17 tonight. For now I want you to take time and ask God to search your heart and ask him to help you make it a habit.

Father I ask that You search my heart. Show me the things I need to see. Let this become a habitual request. I don't want anything between us cluttering our communication. I want to clearly hear Your voice. Give me strength to hear what You say and perseverance to repent and turn from sin.

Your turn

Evening

This evening re-read Psalm 17. Notice in verse 12 he describes a lion waiting in ambush for him. Any guesses on who that is? Now verse 13, David asks the Lord to confront him. Just like praise stills the enemy, truth silences Satan's lies. When Satan accuses you and tells you that you are a sinner, it is a lie based on a partial truth. You were a sinner, but you aren't now. You may still sin from time to time, but it no longer defines you. Your name is written in the lamb's book of life. It cannot be taken out. You are exactly who God says you are: His child, an heir with Christ, and nothing Satan can say true, false, or otherwise can change that. When Satan comes to accuse us, we turn and say, "Arise, O Lord, confront him, subdue him!" We don't have to contend with Satan. He has already been contended with. We only remind him of who we really are!

I learned one of the most interesting science facts ever the other day. Did you know that leaves on trees are not actually green. The green is only the presence of chlorophyll. In the fall, when we say the leaves change color, they are actually revealing their true colors. The chlorophyll is no longer present because the trees will not use it for the winter. The leaves actual colors all year are red, yellow, gold, and brilliant orange, we just can't see it. "All creation is waiting eagerly for that future day when God will reveal who his children really are" (Romans 8:19).

God remind us who we really are. When Satan whispers to us, remind us that praise stills our enemy. Remind us of all you made us to be; we have a purpose and a plan. God, the infinite God, loves us with a steadfast love so much that He came back to rescue us. Let this knowledge propel us to crazy love of others and a desire for them to know what we know.

Your turn

additional journaling space…

Morning   Day 5

Read Psalm 40 this morning. David understood that his identity didn't change in any season because it was rooted in the steadfast. His time as a shepherd was not more or less important than his time as King. It was all used by God and that gave it meaning. We don't need to feel the need to make ourselves feel less or more important. If I am being used by God in any season, then my identity does not rest in my role as mother, student, wife, teacher, leader, follower, CEO, encourager, etc….the list can go on and on. It isn't our identity. Our identity rests in who God is.

The world always pulls us from this, telling us who we should or shouldn't be. Everywhere we look we are being asked to identify ourselves by things that don't really define us. The world seeks to find worth in their identity, because all they have is themselves. We have so much more. They have this life and all they can make it. For us this life isn't it. These views lead to very different conclusions of identity. It leads the world to a place of hopelessness and us to a place of hopefulness.

"Blessed is the man who makes the Lord his trust", not in himself, or what he does, who he is, or what he has.

Show me how the world tries to identify me and let me put no hope in it. You have set my feet upon a rock and put a song of praise in my mouth. Let the people who see it, know that it was You and let them grow to trust You. God, as for me I am poor and needy, but I am never too needy for You. You multiply your wonders and thoughts toward me, it is a wonder that I ever cross Your mind. Let your steadfast love and faithfulness ever preserve me. Show me how the world tries to identify me and let me put no hope in it.

Your turn

additional journaling space…

Evening

Read Psalm 40 again tonight but first pray that it falls on a fresh heart. See what you notice about verses 9&10.

While you journal tonight, ask God how you can be more identified with Him so that the world can identify Him in you.

You are not ashamed of us, which is a constant amazement to me. In fact you trust us to be Your identity to the world. Let our lips not be restrained no matter how large our audience. Don't let me hide your deliverance only in my heart. Let it never be said that I concealed your steadfast love out of fear that it would change my identity to the world.

While you journal tonight, ask God how you can be more identified with Him so that the world can identify Him in you.

Your turn

WEEK 4

Sin

"For the law of the Spirit of life has set you free in Christ Jesus from the law of sin and death."
Romans 8:2

"The freer the man, the stronger the bond that binds him to Him who made his freedom."
George MacDonald

Introduction to Week 4

Sin

Sin at its core is deception and we fight it just like any other lie, by putting up the truth and exposing it to the Light. Satan uses deception instead of a flat out lie because it is a distortion of the truth so it is easier to believe. The danger comes when there are parts of us, our lives, which are not exposed to the Light. God cannot be compartmentalized. If we leave him out of any area of our lives, we are giving Satan wiggle room.

Satan is out to trick us. He will beguile us by any means possible. He uses deception because it is easy to fall for. We are called to be on alert and be constantly exposing ourselves to God's light. Proverbs 3:6 says, "In all your ways acknowledge him, and he will make straight your paths." That word acknowledge is the Hebrew word "yada" which means, "to know with certainty as with intimate friends". David constantly speaks in the psalms of being found innocent and being true. He speaks of his righteousness and upright heart. How could he say these things? He could say them because he kept in fellowship with God, they had an intimate relationship. He did not let time pass without God searching his heart; every part of his heart was exposed to God. Open communication in the form of frequent prayers; keep us in step with God. We fall in to trouble when we stray from that dependence.

David was not a man without sin. He knew that. His relationship with God fell out of step because he wasn't where he was supposed to be. It didn't happen just one night on a rooftop. David took his eyes off God and fell idle. He was not actively seeking to keep in step with God. 2

Samuel 11:1 says, "In the spring of the year, the time when kings go out to battle, David sent Joab, and his servants with him, and all Israel. And they ravaged the Ammonites and besieged Rabbah. But David remained at Jerusalem". Did you notice the phrase, "when the kings go out to war"? It's what kings do, lead the troops. David didn't go to battle. He quit. He became idle, and if there is one thing I have learned it's that an idle mind is ripe for an idol. David put down his sword and Satan took full advantage of it. We can learn from David that if we are engaged in our battle, our eyes are less likely to wander.

Morning   Day 1

David was a man of God who accomplished an incredible amount as King of Israel. He was called a man after God's own heart, but it wasn't because of his lack of sin. He isn't unique in this; many of the men and women God uses have had their share of heinous sins. What makes him unique is his response to sin. When confronted, he didn't try to hide or make excuses; he dealt with it. Read 2 Samuel 12:1-9.

Now read Psalm 51, it was written right after Nathan the prophet came to convict David of his sin with Bathsheba, and the murder of her husband.

David appeals to God's mercy and steadfast love. He knows that he blew it and let go of all that held him fast! So what does he appeal to, the thing that held him fast...steadfast love and mercy.

In verse 8 he asks that the bones God has broken would rejoice. According to Jon Courson's Application Commentary, "This verse is a reference to what a shepherd does when a sheep strays. The shepherd breaks its legs and carries the lamb on his shoulders. As the weeks go by, the lamb develops such a close bond with the shepherd that, when its legs are healed, it never strays from the shepherd again." David needed to be broken so that humility could work in him. God's discipline of David was his mercy and steadfast love toward David. God's discipline *is* His mercy toward us because it saves us from ourselves. We need the discipline of God to keep us where we belong, by His side. We need to cry out with David, "...let the bones you have broken rejoice...create in me a clean heart ...renew a steadfast spirit in me" (verses 8&10). We need to rejoice in God's discipline and His steadfast love for us. It is our constant and it is all that keeps us from ourselves and certain failure.

In the same way, we are responsible to discipline our children. It is a mercy to them. It is our God given job to save them from themselves. When we do not discipline, we reap what we sow in an unruly household, but they also suffer the consequences. They will follow an undisciplined path and life will be harder for them in the long run. That is the reason we have so many undisciplined adults, our society has bought into the lie that childhood is a time to just have fun and be a kid. No wonder we have so many adults who don't understand there are consequences for their actions!

God I ask that you discipline me in your mercy and steadfast love. Teach me to rejoice in my healing and brokenness because it brings me close to the shepherd. Let my brokenness be a sacrifice that you do not despise. Renew in me a steadfast spirit. Restore the joy of your salvation and uphold me with a willing spirit to choose what is right.

If you have children, this is a great prayer to pray over them.

Your turn

Evening

Read Psalm 32

We learned this morning that our proximity to the Steadfast fixes what is broken. Think on that when you read verses 8&9.

Father let me be quick to acknowledge my sin to you and not try to cover my iniquity.
God let me respond to your instruction, teach me the way I should go. Thank you that your eye is upon me. I pray that I will not need a bit and bridle to curb me and keep me near You. Uphold me with a willing spirit to stay close to You (Psalm 51). Thank you that I am blessed because my transgressions are forgiven and You count no iniquity against me.

Your turn

Morning   Day 2

First, read 2 Samuel 12:13-23. These are the consequences that God allowed because of David's sin. This was the breaking of him so that he would wander from the shepherd no more. In God's mercy everything in me believes that during this time, He kept David close to his heart.

I admire David so for his trust of God's decision and his hope that God would change His mind at the same time. When God said no, and the baby died, David got up. He didn't wallow, he didn't distrust God; he simply got up. He expected good from the Lord, and even when God's good and David's expectation didn't match, David rested in it. He went on knowing that one day, "I shall go to him, but he will not return to me." (2 Samuel 12:23). His hope was in heaven.

David understood and accepted God's character and promises. He did not find steadfast to be a quality that inspired fear, but rather stability. "For the King trusts in the Lord, and through the steadfast love of the Most High he shall not be moved" (Psalm 21:7).
What made him "not move" is that he spent seven days prior to this event seeking God (v.16). He anchored himself to the steadfast and that is all that held him when the wave hit. He spent seven days with nothing but God. Prayer allows God to prepare us for the future without our knowing it. It opens the door for His Spirit to work. Prayer is a refining process; it purifies our intentions.

Now read Psalm 39.

"And now, O Lord, for what do I wait?
My hope is in you.
Deliver me from all my transgressions.
Do not make me the scorn of the fool!
I am mute; I do not open my mouth,
for it is you who have done it."

Now, underline the question in these verses. Is there something else other than God that you are waiting for? Is there deliverance or an answered prayer that you are waiting for God to answer the way you desire? Ask God to direct your hope to Him and not the answered prayer. It may be that God gives exactly what you are asking, or it may be that God directs your hope to Him alone. He will be faithful. David understood how sovereign God was over his circumstances. What we can see from David's response is not his strength, but a steadfast God who upheld him.

God give me the strength I need to accept what comes from Your hand. Reel me in so that I may feel Your stability when I am about to topple. Hold not your peace at my tears and at the same time let me remember that I am a mere breath. Thank you that when consequences of sin come, You do not turn from us but draw closer. Remind me that my hope is in you, I have no other.

Your turn

Evening

David did not wallow in his sin and he chose to believe what God said about him. David chose to believe he was forgiven and that made all the difference in the rest of his life. David chose to believe the truth and not the lie Satan tried to feed him, that his sin counted him out and God was done using him.

Read Psalm 103. Now let's look more closely at verses 8-13.

8 The Lord is merciful and gracious,
slow to anger and abounding in steadfast love.
9 He will not always chide,
nor will he keep his anger forever.
10 He does not deal with us according to our sins,
nor repay us according to our iniquities.
11 For as high as the heavens are above the earth,
so great is his steadfast love toward those who fear him;
12 as far as the east is from the west,
so far does he remove our transgressions from us.
13 As a father shows compassion to his children,
so the Lord shows compassion to those who fear him.

After talking about the consequences of our sin, I am refreshed to hear that the Lord does not deal with us according to our sins nor repay us according to our iniquity. The punishment for sin is death, and in Christ none of us will have to pay that penalty. Hallelujah! We will not be separated from God because of His steadfast love! When He has forgiven us our sin, He remembers it no more (Isaiah 43:25). He removes it as far as the East is from the West. Something this magnificent deserves some time to praise God.

God I can't thank you enough for how You deal with us as a father. You only allow us to be broken so that we run home. You have set us free, and in that you give us a purpose. God let the fact that I have been forgiven much cause me to forgive much. Thank You that You daily bear us up.

"Blessed be the Lord, who daily bears us up."
Psalm 68:19

Your turn

Morning   Day 3

Read Psalm 26

David amazes me because of his ability to grasp his forgiven state in God's eyes. Not only did He trust God's ways he believed His words and lived in them. He believed that God loved him and that he was a new creature. David could say that he "trusted in the Lord without wavering" (v.1) because he understood that his mistakes did not count him out. It was because of them that he trusted and that he could say, "prove me, try me, test my heart" (v.2). He knew that God looked on him as a new creature with no sin. Few, if any of us, grasp this. I admit in my own heart that even writing it I feel a doubt try to spring up. But it is true. If any of us are in Christ we are a new creation (2 Corinthians 5:17). There is no condemnation for us if we are found in Jesus (Romans 8:1). God does not identify us by our sins, only we do. The reason for David's ability to grasp this truth is in verse 3, 'For your steadfast love is before my eyes, and I walk in your faithfulness". He fixed his eyes on God's steadfast love and then walked on in God's faithfulness.

Father, I ask that You prove me, try me, and test me. Give me courage to face anything that needs dealt with. Help me lay down that baggage that ties me to earth so that I can be that much closer to You. God I pray that you would set my eyes on your steadfast love for me until everything else fades. Then I can walk on, not ever looking down and proclaiming thanksgiving aloud.

Your turn

Evening

Read Psalm 122 & 124…don't worry they're short. These are both psalms of ascent, they were sung by pilgrims on their way up to the temple. In Psalm 122:2 David says, "our feet have been standing within your gates". When people entered the temple they first went inside the gates where the courtyard was. I think David's hearts cry was that he didn't want to just stay inside the gate, he wanted into the sanctuary. He wanted to give thanks and worship. His prayer was for "peace within you". David meant the city of Jerusalem; but I think it can apply to peace within us because we are free. We are free of guilt. Jesus paid the price for our sin, which means not only do we not suffer the wages of sin and death, but we don't have to feel guilt. If we are feeling guilty over sin we have confessed, Satan is trying to keep us just outside the temple, almost to freedom in Christ. I cannot miss the opportunity to tell you again, "there is no condemnation in Christ!!!" (Romans 8:1) My heart's cry is that I will not settle for inside the gates! It is for freedom Christ has set us free! (Galatians 5:1, John 8:36). You are stamped forgiven right on your forehead and nothing can take it off. We confess our sins to God so that we are agreeing with Him and restoring our relationship, but forgiven is something you continually are.

Now think on what Psalm 124 says, "If it had not been for the Lord", the flood would have swept us away and we would not have escaped! Praise God we are forgiven!

Father thank you for my standing in Christ let it bind me closer to You. Let it never be taken for granted and when Satan comes to tell me I am guilty, let me answer him: "Jesus paid it all, all to Him I owe".

Your turn

Morning   Day 4

This morning read Psalm 41. David knew that his sin, terrible as it may have been, and our sin, awful as it is, no longer separates us from God. People were saying of David, "he will not rise again from where he lies." (v.8). In essence they thought David could no longer be used of God. He wouldn't get over this. I couldn't help but think that that is exactly what Satan thought about Jesus. But He did rise again! Hallelujah! Death could not keep him, and because of Him, death cannot keep us.

Let's look at verse 10, "be gracious to me and raise me up that I may <u>repay</u> them." The word "repay" is the Hebrew word "shalem" which means, "to be complete, to restore or finish". Stay with me here, David wants to repay his enemies by showing them his restoration or completeness. That is exactly how we repay Satan. The enemy of our soul comes to us and attacks our standing to make us doubt our standing in Christ, and we repay him by showing him God's restoration. We say to Satan, you thought I was down, but God has made me whole. I have been restored. Again in verse 12 David says God upheld him because of his integrity. This made me think about integrity and why David would say this. So I dug again and found that the word integrity in this verse is the Hebrew word "tamam" meaning, "to be complete or finished", even suggesting that it was consumed. As Hebrews 12:29 reminds us, our God is a consuming fire. David's sin was dealt with, God upheld him according to what Jesus completed or finished on the cross. The sin in him was consumed by the Holiness of God.

In this same way God upholds us. We also are completed in Jesus. We can say to Satan, the sin you designed to destroy me has served to propel me to God's feet and He has finished it. That is how Satan is repaid. We show him the work of God in us. When Satan desires our separation from God, we cling all the more to Him! That is how we advance on the battle field. That is how we repay.

God is faithful to love us with a perfect love that consumes in us what is against us in our own flesh. We should run to God, without fear, that He might consume in us what will certainly harm us if left alone. George

MacDonald says, "The man whose deeds are evil, fears the burning. But the burning will not come the less that he fears it or denies it. Escape is hopeless. For Love is inexorable. Our God is a consuming fire…for that which cannot be shaken shall remain….The wrath will consume what they call themselves; so that the selves God made shall appear". God is the only force that can consume without damaging. He alone can burn without tearing down but actually making new.

Father I pray that You will continue to consume in me what needs consumed. That it will not make me fear You, but cling to You instead. Thank you that our sin does not count us out. Rather, in restoration it can be used by a Holy God to repay Satan. I want to bring You glory.

Your turn

Evening

So tonight we are going to revisit Psalm 51. Let's look more closely at these verses:

7 Purge me with hyssop, and I shall be clean;
wash me, and I shall be whiter than snow.
8 Let me hear joy and gladness;
let the bones that you have broken rejoice.
9 Hide your face from my sins,
and blot out all my iniquities.
10 Create in me a clean heart, O God,
and renew a right spirit within me.
11 Cast me not away from your presence,
and take not your Holy Spirit from me.
12 Restore to me the joy of your salvation,
and uphold me with a willing spirit.
13 Then I will teach transgressors your ways,
and sinners will return to you.

Go back and circle the word "Then". What was the result of David's sin and restoration? Once God had purged, washed, and healed his broken bones; he could renew a right spirit and restore the joy of salvation. God upheld him with a willing spirit so that he could teach others. And the ultimate goal; sinners will return to God. David allowed God to work humility in him. Then David became an arrow to strike right at the heart of Satan. What Satan planned for David, God took and redeemed. We so often think that our sin counts us out. That is exactly what Satan wants... don't give it to him.

Father, restore the joy of your salvation and take not Your Holy Spirit from me. Let me be consumed so that I can be used to show Your steadfast love to sinners who need to return home. Don't let me believe Satan when he tries to remind me of my guilt and tell me I am no longer in the battle. Let me lay aside every weight and sin which clings so closely (Hebrews12:1).

"Jesus paid it all,
All to Him I owe,
Sin had left a crimson stain
He washed it white as snow."

Your turn

Morning   Day 5

Now we go on the offense! David was a man of action; he knew battle. We may not go to war with physical weapons, but we have weapons. We just don't use them enough! One of the best weapons we have is prayer. We are not in this alone. Prayer is calling for reinforcements! We have the best at our disposal! We are not supposed to brave it alone.

Read Psalm 70. Not only did David call God for help, he said Hurry Up! Make haste to help me. We need to do this as soon as we feel the pull of sin on us. If we let it linger, it grows. Ask for help immediately.

Now read Psalm 101. "I will walk with integrity of heart within my house; I will not set before my eyes anything that is worthless" (v. 2&3). This is a powerful offensive plan! David knew the power of what you set your eyes on, he learned first hand how dangerous it can be. He set his eyes on Bathsheba from his own rooftop. The home is a place of comfort, but the familiar can wreak havoc. We don't always recognize sin once it has become comfortable. Read Psalm 101:8 again. When is David planning on destroying the wicked…Morning by Morning…it's a repeat process! To destroy sin in us, it is a repeat process, morning by morning.

Pen your prayer to God and ask Him to show you what you are setting before your eye that is worthless. That is a key word - worthless. It doesn't have to be clearly evil to be worthless. We are to set our mind on whatever is true, whatever is honorable, whatever is just, whatever is pure, whatever is lovely, whatever is commendable, if there is any excellence, if there is anything worthy of praise think on these things (Philippians 4:8).
What is worthless in light of eternity? If it has no eternal significance does it have worth?
Remember that what is most real to us is what we fix our hearts on, or our eyes.

God search me in my home. Show me what has become comfortable and unnoticed. Let me fix my eyes only on things that are worthy in eternity. Don't let me define my goodness by the world's standards. Only You are holy. Make me different than my culture so that it is noticeable and can be used to draw souls to You.

Your turn

Evening

Tonight read the following scripture excerpts:

Psalm 144:1, "Blessed be the Lord, my rock, who trains my hands for war and my fingers for battle."

Psalm 55:18, "He redeems my soul in safety from the battle that I wage, for many are arrayed against me."

Psalm 140:7, "O Lord, my Lord, the strength of my salvation, you have covered my head in the day of battle."

God will not allow a fatal blow to your soul! It is safe. He does not send us out into battle defenseless. According to Ephesians 6 we have a helmet. God knows without your head, you can't win a battle. If we are going to wage war on sin in us, we have to keep our heads. The mind is a powerful weapon. To use it, we must have it clear and focused. Prayerful praise refocuses us on who God is! We have to start thinking like we have the upper hand, because we do, God is on our side.

Father remind me that I am on the winning side. Focus my mind on You, thank you for the helmet of salvation that assures me I will not be lost. Help me to not put anything worthless before my eyes so that my mind is uncluttered and I am not distracted when the enemy comes. Train me for battle because that is what I was intended for. I want to wage war in prayer. Don't allow me to sit on the bench because I am not a threat! I want to be a threat!

Your turn

Week 5

No Fear

"Because He lives, I can face tomorrow
Because He lives, all fear is gone
Because I know He holds the future
And life is worth the living, just because He lives."

Bill Gaither

Introduction to Week 5

No Fear

All fear finds its roots in insecurity. We crave security; it gives us a false sense of control. But no matter how hard we try to grasp for control of the people and circumstances in our lives, we are not in control. David was a man who did not let himself be controlled by fear, not the fear of man or fear of circumstances. He believed what God said. He knew who God was, and he viewed the world from these truths. In psalm 56:9 he says, "This I know, that God is for me". Can you say that; can you mean it?

If God is for me, then it can't matter if anyone else is. Man's favor cannot factor into the decisions I make. Man is limited and God is unlimited. The favor of man is fleeting while the favor of God is forever! There is no comparison. We are constantly disappointed in this life because of the expectations we put on man. Great clarity comes by following God alone. If God alone is who we respect and fears above all others, our minds are not clouded by many counselors and opinions.

Knowing that God is for me does not mean that nothing bad will ever happen to me. Most people really do believe that if they don't do anything terrible, nothing *really* bad will happen to them. They may not confess this with their mouth, but it is how they function. Our problem is our definition of "bad". What we see as bad is often a gift. The problem is we aren't willing to receive it. It takes away our pseudo security. When "bad" happens it forces our eyes off the shifting sands to search for something steadfast. In that is the gift.

Fear has always been a big thing for me. I come from a long line of fear, but no one could ever help me deal with fear. Countless people would try to comfort me by telling me that what I feared would never happen to me. However, even as a child I knew they couldn't know that. Our approach to dealing with fear cannot be to rationalize it away. In this world horrible things do happen. If we cannot rationalize fear away then we have to learn how to handle it.

Whether we fear the approval of man or ever changing circumstances the answer to both fears is the same. We set our eyes on the person of steadfast love, because He alone doesn't change and we walk on in His faithfulness. He alone can keep us steady as the world shifts all around us. "Set his steadfast love before your eyes, then walk on in His faithfulness" (Psalm 26:3). How do we set our eyes on steadfast love? We set God always before us, His word, music that speaks His promises, people who speak truth to us, and prayer every five minutes if need be. It may not sound practical, but neither is living in fear.

Morning   *Day 1*

Read 1 Samuel 24:8-10 for a little history on how Saul dealt with the fear of man. Saul listened to the opinions of men more than the word of God. He was swayed by their constantly changing emotions which made him unstable.

Now Read 1Samuel 14:52, when Saul found any strong man he attached them to himself. I would imagine with bribes, flattery, and much manipulation. In contrast men flocked to David. He was a man with faults, but he could be trusted because he was not led by his fear of man. He had a track record from early on of not being swayed by the opinions of men. He leaned on a steadfast God, and other men saw the affect that had on David. It made him steadfast as well, a man to be trusted.

Now in contrast to Saul's response to the pressure of man, read 1Samuel 30:1-9. Did you notice that David strengthened himself in God and then he waited for what God would say to do? Never mind that the people were talking of stoning him! Talk about strength from God. That took serious self-control, and self-control is a fruit of the spirit (Galatians 5:22). We are incapable of it without the indwelling of the Holy Spirit. David was a man who lived by the spirit. Even under great stress he sought God's will over man's advice.

Lastly, I promise, read 1 Samuel 13:8-15. When Saul saw the people getting restless he feared them more than God and he made his own path. When Samuel arrived he announced that God was done with Saul and had chosen another, "a man after his own heart" (v.14), a man who didn't fear men. What did Saul do in verse 15? He numbered the people. He relied on the strength of the people more than God. In contrast, David inspired fearlessness because he believed God. He was the kind of guy who inspired confidence because of his confidence in God. He knew only God was to be feared.

Read Psalm 130. David waits, but did you notice what he does while waiting? "I wait for the Lord, my soul waits, and <u>in his word I hope</u>" (v.5).

When we are asked to wait, what do we do? Is our first reaction to take hope in His word? Do you recall his promises and then watch? Think about how a watchman waits for the morning. They have been up all night, and they are waiting for the first sign of their rest, never taking their eyes off the horizon wanting to catch the first glimpse of sunrise.

God teach me that when I wait for You to come to my rescue, I should go straight to Your word and renew my hope. Let me continue steadfastly in prayer, being watchful in it with thanksgiving (Colossians 4:2). Remind me that thanksgiving reminds me of Your faithfulness and that produces hope.

Your turn…

Evening

This evening read Psalm 11. "How can you say to my soul flee like a bird to your mountain…what can the righteous do?" (v.1). Most commentators agree that this was written while David was on the run from Saul. His response to the threats of the wicked "who shoot in the dark at the upright in heart" is: God is still watching. He hasn't missed all this. He isn't abandoning us now. Jon Courson's Application Commentary calls this psalm "Faith's response to fear's advice".

I don't know about you but doesn't shooting in the dark at the upright sound like something Satan does. Sometimes Satan can use man to shoot in the dark at us; especially if it's a friend, because we don't see it coming. The person being used may not intend that at all, but their words can bring doubt to your heart. Jesus rebuked Peter in Matthew 16:23 for telling him that what the Lord had willed would not be. Rather than encouraging Jesus faith in the Father, Peter, probably out of his own fear, did not want to accept it.

People who seem fearless are not people who fear little. Rather, they are people who fear a lot, but all they hear is the cry of the lover of their soul. David inspired fearlessness in men because he reminded them that the only voice worth hearing is God's.

God let Your voice be all I hear. I won't turn back.

Your turn

Morning   Day 2

Read Psalm 23 with a fresh heart & receive it anew. I love how *The Message* phrases several parts. If you have this translation, give it a try this morning.

This psalm has a deep personal meaning to me. It is the first psalm my daughter committed to memory. It is burned into mine. On April 28, 2011 at about 12:45 in the a.m. we said it from memory as we crouched together in our pantry while our home was being taken apart by an F4 tornado. Lots of people have asked me if it was the scariest thing I had ever imagined. (Clearly these were people who didn't know how active an imagination I have). So many people remarked afterwards how calm I was. They attributed it to shock, but I don't think that was it at all. It was the presence of my shepherd. He never left us. In those moments that felt like eternity, He was there. I am not saying that as a recollection that He must have been. I mean I *know* He was there. I wasn't as afraid as I had always imagined I would be, because I couldn't have imagined His presence like that until I needed it. In the shadow of our valley there was light. You know I really can't remember it being dark, even though I know the power was out. Fear's power is the unknown. There is nothing God doesn't know, so fear has no power over Him, and it only has power over us if we let it. That doesn't mean we don't feel it.

Our tornado was a gift to me. I have been terrified of tornadoes since the 4th grade, and at the age of 32 what I had long feared *did* happen. God used that specific fear to get a message to my heart. It wasn't coincidence; it was personal. He used my very personal fear to say to my heart, "See what you feared happened, and I never left". What could have seemed terrible, that God let the thing I have long feared happen, was actually love. 1 John 4:18 tells us," There is no fear in love, for fear has to do with punishment, the one who fears has not been perfected in love". Perfect love is the person of Jesus. In the process of making me perfect we had to walk that tornado together. Now the task I have is remembering to surrender my fears and to continually be made perfect in love. To do that, I have to continually tell them to God, and then praise Him for His perfect love.

I think David would have experienced so much of God's presence as a shepherd that it was a habit to stay in close contact with God. That made all the difference in his fears. David experienced some really scary things, and they were God's gifts to him. They were a reminder of his continual presence and they reminded David of his continual need for it.
Confess the fears that you are feeling right now to God and ask Him to be present in them. Ask Him to be made perfect in love.

Father I cannot thank you enough for the gift that was our tornado. Don't let me ever forget that You are not done with me; You have a purpose for me every minute I am kept on this earth. Thank you that I have nothing to fear because I have perfect love. I have a shepherd who goes with me even in the darkest valley. In that darkness His light shines that much brighter.

Your turn

Evening

This evening read Psalm 20 and then pray it over yourself, plugging in your name. Now pray it over someone you love. Prayer is the best action of love we can take for another person. It brings perfect love Himself to the situation. George MacDonald said, "And why should the good of anyone depend on the prayer of another? I can only answer with the return question, why should my love be powerless to help another?"

Father, help us never forget that You are more clearly seen when we are in trouble. Send us help from the sanctuary and support that we need. Remember our offerings; help us to be quick to offer belief and trust. Fulfill our plans as they come from a right heart that is rejoicing in your salvation. Let our success wear the banner that proclaims the name of the Lord our God. Thank You for always answering us when we call.

Your turn

Morning   Day 3

Read Psalm 25. David was comfortable without man's approval. He could tune out their voices and focus in on the One he needed to hear. He could wait for the Lord without fearing that he would be put to shame. God had proved himself over and over. Doesn't God do that with us? And still when He asks us to go out on a limb for Him, we fear that we will be put to shame in our hope (Psalm 25:2, 3, &20). Quite honestly it isn't always about our own image, somewhere deep inside we fear that God will somehow be put to shame through us. We fear sharing our convictions out loud because if we are wrong, we fear that will make God wrong. God is never wrong. David could know that he would not be put to shame because he put his hope in God and not the ideal of how he thought God could work out the circumstances. David said, "for you I will wait all the day long" (Psalm 25:5). He knew God would come through; even if he had no idea what it would look like. That is where we err. We want to know what it will look like before we trust. "All the paths of the Lord are steadfast love and faithfulness" (Psalm 25:10), even if it is not the path we assumed, we can trust it will be the right one. We will not be put to shame in our hope!

The more our eyes are ever toward the Lord (Psalm 25:15), the less we will look around to see what man thinks.

To You and You alone may I lift up my soul! Let me not be put to shame, remember me for the sake of Your goodness. Instruct me in the way that I should choose and when I doubt remind me that all the paths of the Lord are steadfast love and faithfulness.

Your turn

Evening

Read Psalm 109. This psalm is a response to the betrayal of Ahithophel in 2 Samuel 15. It is also prophetic of the betrayal of Judas. Peter alludes to it in Acts 1:20. Some commentaries believe that this is a picture of David's humanity, calling down curses on those who betrayed him, but I agree with those who think that David is listing the things that were said against him. You can read and decide, but what I want you to note is David's response to the attacks and accusations in verse 4, "but I give myself to prayer". Instead of feeling the need to justify himself or defend himself, he gave himself to prayer and asked God to "deal on my behalf for your name's sake; because your steadfast love is good, deliver me!" (Psalm 109:21). He didn't ask God to redeem his own name, but to do this for God's name's sake. That God may have glory in it, "that they would know that this is your hand; you, O Lord, you have done it!" (Psalm 109:27). David chooses not to retaliate. Instead of doing harm with his mouth, David says, "with my mouth I will give great thanks to the Lord; I will praise him in the midst of the throng" (Psalm 109:30).

God, I pray for the strength to choose praise over retaliation. Let my first reaction to all assaults be to give myself to prayer. Let us remember to be steadfast in prayer and watch for your answer with thanksgiving. Thank you that you are identified with us. You are our defense when we have no other.

Your turn

Morning   Day 4

Read Psalm 15. We already talked about how David felt safe expressing himself to God. He could lay it all out there trusting that God was big enough to take it. He could trust that God judged only his heart and would not misunderstand his words. That is why God is the best person to take our feelings to. We women could take a lesson from this. We feel the need to express our emotions to everyone and then fear being misunderstood or judged. When God is your confidant; He keeps you from sin. Only He can tame the tongue (James 3:8). I am not saying that you can never share feelings with a friend or ask for prayer, but you should only do this after talking to God first. This will keep you from sinning with your lips.

As women, we sometimes feel this need to shield God from our emotions and not show him our sorrow or anger. It makes no sense because He knows our thoughts before we have them. For some reason we think that if we just deny the thought it isn't true. That is the same logic as going to the doctor with a broken arm and then saying, "Don't put it in a cast, I am sure it will be fine if we pretend it isn't hurt". What we should actually do is lay them all out before God and say, "You deal with these, heal them and make them right". He is the only one who understands our needs and motives perfectly and not only can He understand them, He can fix them. Instead of letting them fester, we need to take them to the Physician who can heal them.

Now look at verses 3&4 again. The Lord hears when I ponder in my own heart. When I am angry, hurt, or unforgiving; I can take that to God. He can judge those emotions rightly. We can trust that we have been heard, and the situation is in the hands of the One who can heal it. He can fill our need to be understood and healed at the same time. This keeps us from sinning with our lips. David understood this truth. He could trust God with his feelings and God would redirect his thoughts. This kept him from sin. It also gave him stability. People crave stability. He could lead men because his stability did not depend on his feelings. We can only lead the hearts of men to Jesus when they see our stability is based on God's steadfast love rather than our feelings or reactions.

In closing, read Psalm 15: 1-3. Have you ever taken up a reproach against your friend? In Hebrew "take up" is translated "receive". Now let me ask that again, have you ever received a reproach against a friend? That means joined in with someone else's slander of a person, or in fear of being disliked remaining silent and not coming to the defense of a friend? That hits home a little more, huh? Not only should we not slander others, we shouldn't participate in any way when others are slandering! If David practiced this, no wonder men flocked to him. He could be trusted! He didn't speak rashly in anger; he took those feelings to God. He didn't slander others or listen to the slander of others. Anytime we speak rashly someone is sure to be hurt. We are wise to practice running everything that comes out of our mouth past the ears of God first.

O God, I want to dwell in your tent. Teach me to speak truth even in my heart. See into it and cleanse it that truth flow out of it. Let me not slander with my tongue; let it rather be and instrument of healing. Let it bring grace to those who hear (Ephesians 4:29). Let me never be moved because you hold me fast.

Your turn

Evening

Read Psalm 141. Talk about discernment. David knew his own mouth was a danger. He also understood the balance between words meant to hurt and hard words meant to heal. Check out verse 5 again. He knew that a righteous rebuke should not be refused.

A good prayer to commit to memory is Psalm 141:3 "Set a guard, O Lord, over my mouth; keep watch over the door of my lips!"

God, thank You that You know our hearts. Set a guard over our mouths. They can get us into so much trouble. Let us also have discernment to accept hard words from the righteous and to know when we should be brave enough to rebuke. Let us cling to you to know the difference and not to man's advice.

Your turn

Morning   Day 5

Read Psalm 6. Notice how in verse 4 David petitions the Lord, "save me for the sake of your steadfast love." David goes on to say that in death he could no longer praise God. I think we fear what being saved for the sake of steadfast love will mean. Sometimes our real fear is not that God will ever leave us, but we fear what God will ask of us. We want a life of contentment without problems and fears; we don't want a battle. If that is the life we lead, then God's steadfast love can't be seen in us. Remember I said that we can't be steadfast if nothing ever tries to move us. I want to be steadfast, but so many times I need the desire to take what comes against me willingly, so that God can use it for the sake of steadfast love.

David looked at battles as an opportunity for God to show off. He prayed continually to be delivered, so I am not saying that we should not pray for deliverance. We just need to be willing to battle in prayer for deliverance. Quite frankly it doesn't need to be a life threatening instance, it can just be a day, a 24 hour span of time that we desire to do battle, to stand against the schemes of the devil, to hold fast and not go with the tide. We need courage to do battle against sin because it is crouching at our door and it is real. We need to do battle for our family in prayer, so that they may be saved in God's name and for His glory. That is what continuing steadfastly in prayer means. It isn't a casual thing, it's a battle.

Here are some great battle prayers that can be applied to specific battles or the daily mundane battle:

But you, O God my Lord, deal on my behalf for your name's sake; because your steadfast love is good, deliver me! Psalm 109:21

For your name's sake, O LORD, preserve my life! In your righteousness bring my soul out of trouble! Psalm 143:11

God, deal on my behalf, fight for me, and give me the courage to use the tools you have given for me to fight in prayer. Give me the desire to do battle against the world and against my own flesh. Help me to gain ground for Your name's sake.

Your turn

Evening

Tonight read Psalm 144. The armor of God found in Ephesians 6 is not for a walk in the park, but for a battle. I am thankful that God trains our hands for war and our fingers for battle. He doesn't allow anything that He hasn't equipped us for first (Hebrews 13:21 & Philippians 2:13).

I am also thankful that battle is not all we face. We are also to pray for things like the ones requested at the end of this psalm. Go back and look at verses 12-15. David prays for blessing on children and crops and that granaries be full. We are free to request blessings from God for his name's sake too. We are wise to pray that we will give Him just as much glory for these and that He will be seen in our blessings. Practicing thankfulness keeps our eyes fixed where they should remain.

Thank you that you are my shield and in You I take refuge. Train my hands for war, because I have an enemy and the more I obey the more he will attack. Don't let me go about daily with blinders on, open my eyes to the spiritual battles that are raging all around me. Remind me not to fear because You are my shield and refuge. Give me a desire for Your glory.

Your turn

WEEK 6

Destiny

"We may easily be too big for God to use, but never too small."

D.L.Moody

Introduction to Week 6

Destiny

According to C.S. Lewis, "If you think of this world as a place intended simply for your happiness, you find it quite intolerable. Think of it as a place of training and correction and it's not so bad". God is in the business of making things new. That includes us, if we are still on earth and breathing, He is working on us. God has a secret destiny in place for each of us, "His secret purpose framed from the very beginning is to bring us to our full glory" (1 Corinthians 2:7 NEB). That is our destiny. We are here to be made fit for heaven. That is the end goal, the destiny He desires for us. All of the circumstances in our life are the catalyst that propels us to our destiny, full glory in Christ.

David understood what his destiny was really about. He understood that his circumstances, in the hands of God, serve to accomplish God's purposes. David understood that being King was not his right. It was only a part of his role as long as God ordained that as a plan for bringing David to full glory.

David could look to his past and see how God had prepared him for Kingship with years as a shepherd, living on the run in caves, and watching Saul's demise so that he could lead men well and out of humility. Those seasons in his life were God's gifts. Those things were preparation, but David could not have grasped their importance while in those seasons. Our seasons are God's preparation. Try as we might, we cannot know what God is preparing us for. But we can be sure that our destiny, the one that matters, is secure in heaven. We can be sure that every part of our lives here will accomplish the purpose for which He set it into motion.

Psalm 31:15 says, "My times are in your hands". I love how the *Message* translation phrases it, "Hour by hour I place my days in your hand". This translation makes it much more practical for me. I need to refocus and place my day back in God's hands. Once in the morning doesn't cut it for me. If I do not purposefully redirect my thoughts to the truth, the lies creep in and get believable. When I am tuned in to God, there is not a moment wasted. Every hour we give Him, He will use. Every hour we are conscious of our true destiny and what our reality really is is an hour that can be used to make us more fit for heaven. We have to learn to cooperate with heavenly eyes. We cannot attain our purpose without being made fit for it. The small and daily *is* our destiny. It is how God gets us to his purpose - full glory. The whole cannot be attained without each of the smaller parts. Each of the small mundane parts of our day, when given to God, are transformed into something beautiful. The more moments you release to God the more beautiful your life becomes.

Morning   Day 1

For background this morning read 1 Samuel 24:1-10. David's heart smote him because he took matters into his own hands. His heart relied on God so much that the moment he went after what man advised, his heart told him it was wrong. Ever felt that in your heart? Did you listen?

Now read Psalm 57. David wrote this after the occurrence we just read. Circle each time the word steadfast is used. I am encouraged that David needed the same reminders I do. When he couldn't understand what God was doing or why he needed to wait, he trusted.

How many times do we manipulate circumstances to make our own plans, or to gain man's favor? Instead of waiting in the shadow of His wings until God fulfils His purpose for us (Psalm 57:1&2), we feel the need to get our hands all over it. We try to make the promises of God fit our timeline. Even in this situation where man would argue that as the anointed of God David had the right to take the throne, David would wait for God to act. He would not manipulate his circumstances to "help" the promises of God.

When we remove our hands and stop wasting valuable time working out the future, God will engineer our circumstances so that the impossible becomes possible, allowing the invisible to be made visible. It isn't ultimately about what happens to us and when; it's about God getting the glory for what happens and when.

I cry out with David that You will be merciful to me and forgive me where I have presumed that I am in control. God show me where my hands do not belong. Smite my heart when I act out of manipulation. You are in control. Show me where I have listened to the lies of man that I need to make the promises of God happen. Hold my right hand tightly that I may not get ahead of You or lag behind. Send out Your steadfast love and faithfulness and make my heart steadfast.

Your turn

Evening

Read Psalm 16. David could say of the Lord, "I have no good apart from You". The Lord was his chosen portion, He could be trusted to hold his lot secure. It is a good practice to ask God to hold our lots secure, even from us when we try to get our hands on it.
George MacDonald sheds great light on the heart of man, "Man finds it hard to get what he wants, because he does not want the best; God finds it hard to give, because He would give the best, and man will not take it."

Father, so often we ask with our lips that You give us Your best, but You know in our heart we mean our best. We want You to make us steadfast but would like to get to tell You how. Forgive us. Fix our hearts, change our desires, and most of all make us steadfast in a world where nothing else is that You would be known. Help us to remember that this is the preparation for heaven

Your turn

Morning   Day 2

This passage encompasses one of the most interesting things I have learned through my study of David. It hit me like a slap in the face…well that makes it sound unpleasant, let's say fresh water on a hot day. Okay, time to get to the point. This Psalm was written when David was in the process of bringing the Ark of the Covenant back from Kirjath-jearim. You've never heard of that name for a reason. The ark was in a little nowhere town. Anyway, to get the history you need, read 1 Samuel 6.

Okay now read Psalm 30. Doesn't the history make it so much more clear what David is feeling? God had hidden his face, and David didn't understand. He learned a really important lesson. You can read 1 Samuel 7 for more information but I will sum up; David had not followed the instructions written down for the transportation of the ark, and as a result one of the men carrying the Ark was struck dead. This caused David's hesitation. He was trying to do something that He knew God wanted, but he did not stop long enough to hear the how.

This is a quote from my very favorite commentary by Jon Courson:

"This time he [David] went back to the Bible, where God declared that the ark was to be carried on the shoulders of the priests (1 Chronicles 15:15). Every six steps, the procession stopped so David could build an alter and offer a sacrifice. Efficiency experts would say that was not the best way to get from the house of Obed-edom to Jerusalem. Efficiency, after all, is doing things right. But God's not interested in efficiency. He's interested in effectiveness – and - effectiveness is doing the right thing. What's the right thing? Six is the number of man, the number of the flesh. Therefore, we need to stop every six steps, every time we feel our flesh well up, and be "altered". We need to stop every six steps to offer the sacrifice of praise, to confess our sin, and to express our dependency upon the Lord. That may not be efficient. But it's guaranteed to be effective."

You thought journaling twice a day was a lot to ask!

Father let me realize my need for You every six steps. Let me learn this kind of prayer that teaches me to cling to You through the day and pulls me back to my anchor. This kind of prayer can make my heart whole, make me whole Jesus. As soon as I start to feel the hole widening, fill it with yourself. Make me effective and redeem me from the oppression of the world which says I need to be efficient.

Your turn

Evening

Read Psalm 61.

Hear my cry, listen to my prayer. When my heart is faint, lead me to the rock that is higher than I. Thank you that You are higher than I and that you can lead me to higher ground. Thank you for giving me the Heritage of those that fear Your name. My heritage is not earthly but heavenly. Appoint steadfast love and faithfulness to watch over me. Let me ever sing praise to Your name. God you are my joy. Let me have joy as I choose to perform my vows to you day after day.

Your turn

Morning   Day 3

David understood that not only was God in charge of his destiny, He was in charge of preparing him for it. Preparation is kind of like packing. You need to know where you are going so that you have the right stuff. Only we don't know where we are going; only God does. We have to rely on him to equip us with what we need. God will…"equip you with everything good that you may do his will, working in us that which is pleasing in his sight, through Jesus Christ, to whom be glory forever and ever. Amen" (Hebrews 13:21). He will equip you so that He can get glory through you. He doesn't pack things just to make you comfortable. David spent a lot of time being uncomfortable, not just physically but emotionally. He lived in caves for an estimated seven years on the run from Saul after he was anointed as King of Israel. It was God's preparation. He had to learn not to fear man but to only fear God, he had to learn that God would do what He said, and he had to learn to wait for God to act. Other ins and outs only God knew, but that is exactly the point. David may not have foreseen this as equipping him at the time. He probably struggled with it being wasted time. Remember effective always trumps efficient. With God there is no waste of time. With God the most important time is the middle, between the promise and the attaining. The end will come regardless, but we cannot miss the details. Battles are won in the days, hours, and minutes. Our destiny isn't just about some end goal. Our destiny is about being made useful for God's purpose. He has engineered all of our days, hours, and minutes to refine us. Our destiny is to be made holy as He is holy.

Now read Psalm 138 and respond in prayer.

We have need of endurance God. There is only one way to get it, like most things worth having it takes work. Pull us into the steadfast so that we may draw our strength from our dependence on You. Increase my strength of soul. Thank you that I have a purpose and that Your steadfast love can produce it in me because that love endures forever. Father, never forsake the work of your hands.

Your turn

Evening

This evening read Psalm 31. If we put our trust in the Lord, we will not be put to shame. As you read this psalm, I want you to circle the "Buts". Remember, it's the "But" that changes everything!

Help me trust You God, my times are in Your hands! Let me not be put to shame because I call upon You, that You may get the glory. Lead me and guide me for your name's sake Give me strength to take courage because I wait for You, and You alone are sure to arrive! You alone are sure as the dawn!

Your turn

Morning   Day 4

My son, Brian, and I were watching a movie the other day. It was a classic, *Kung Foo Panda 2*. Okay not a classic but boys love this kind of movie and, I love that about them. They love the battle. Even with his love of battle Brian, and my other children, are very sensitive to anything scary or evil. My prayer is that they keep this sensitivity in a healthy way, but do not fear evil. The first time we watched this movie the bad guys were a little scary for Brian and I would fast forward the beginning a little. While watching the other day Brian leans over and says to me, "Mom you know why I like this movie so much? It's because I know the end and the good guys win." He was able to watch the sad or scary part because he could watch it in context with the end. I realize that is why I only like movies with happy endings. That is how it is supposed to be. As hard as things may be, when you know sadness will only be for a short time, the ending makes it worth watching. That is why the scariest parts of life become okay. We know the end. We need to remember that the Good Guy wins. He already did. Our destiny is safe in God's hands because he has made our eternal destiny secure.

With this in mind read Psalm 24. This is a prophetic psalm about Jesus return for us. My commentary again made my heart sing about this psalm. It's so good I can hardly wait to share it! "According to temple liturgy, a certain psalm was sung every day of the week. On Monday Psalm 48...... And on Sunday this majestic psalm before us that deals with the coming of the King was sung. Thus, this song would have been sung on the first day of the week as Jesus triumphed over the tomb." Psalm 24 was sung on resurrection Sunday! Doesn't that tickle you pink?

In your journal today respond to Psalm 24 by praising Jesus for being the only One who could ascend that hill and deal with sin. Now I want you to do something that sounds crazy, I want you to open up your doors, even though they may not be ancient, that the King of Glory might come in. Enjoy the fresh air and praise the King of glory because one day He will come! I want to be expecting Him when He does.

It's true what they say about success, it's all in who you know. The Who I know is the I am, the beginning and the end.

Thank you God that You are my end. This life is only a vapor. Help me to fix my mind on You so much that I only have one foot here on earth because the other is anchored in heaven. Let it be my reality!

Your turn

Evening

Tonight read Psalm 138. (We have read it already, but let it fall fresh on your heart).

O God I give thanks to You, let this praise make my heart whole. Increase my strength of soul that I won't fear because I know the end! Thank you that though You are high, You regard the lowly. Thank you that though I walk in the midst of trouble and distractions of the world, You preserve me. No matter what my purpose here is, I can trust You to fulfill it. Your steadfast love endures forever into eternity. Thank you that You have already won, and we can know the end. Thank you that there actually is no end in You.

Your turn

Morning   Day 5

For some background today read 2 Samuel 16: 5-14. This account is often titled, "David Flees Jerusalem". I respectfully disagree. I don't believe he was fleeing, not for a moment. It would be entirely out of character. David was not the fleeing type. He was leaving, but it wasn't out of fear, it was out of humility. Surrounded by his mighty men, he chose to leave and let God have the reigns. He chose not to hold on to a Kingship that may or may not be God's next step. You see he had watched a king do just that. He had seen firsthand how Saul tried to maintain his kingship at any cost. He had personally experienced the devastation of Saul's disobedience. If you have read any of the stories of these men who followed David, you know that they loved him. They stood with him to the end, and they were a force to be reckoned with. They were not intimidated by the young Absalom. They begged David to let them kill Shimei. It is interesting to note that not only did David have mercy on Shimei in this instance, but after David returned to the throne Shimei was pardoned of his offenses.

Read psalm 63 and enjoy. David wrote this Psalm when he was in the wilderness of Judah after fleeing Jerusalem because of Absalom's attempt to overthrow him (2 Samuel 15). His soul was thirsty for God. He was dry of spirit. I love how after verse 2 of Psalm 63, David reminds himself of all the times he has looked upon God in the sanctuary and beheld His power. We need to remember this when we are weary. I know I am quick to forget how much of God's power I have been allowed to see. We can be quick to make a list of things we need done, and that list never ends. We need to be quick to make a list of things God has done, and remind ourselves that *that* list never ends.

I love Psalm 63:4; read it again. I know that I heard this somewhere and for the life of me, I can't remember where. Anyway this illustration isn't mine, but it is so good. David says that in God's name, "he will lift up his hands". Think about a stick up. No really, if someone points a gun at you and says "stick 'em up", what do you do? You raise your hands. It is a universal sign of surrender. David is surrendering to God. While his own son was seeking his life David says, "Okay God I surrender" this is on You, "My soul clings to you; your right hand upholds me". That is David's action, cling to God. It isn't cling to God, and then see what he could do on his own. It is only cling to God.

Today we are going to purpose that we will trust God with our obstacles, big and small. When you start to feel the pressure, remind yourself of when you have seen God's power and raise your hands in surrender.

Father when I feel out of control let my reaction be to lift my hands and say, "it's all You God". Then let my only other action be to cling to You. Let me remember that Praise stills the enemy and this is my act of worship. O God when my soul thirsts and my flesh faints, when I am in a dry and weary land, why am I so quick to forget of my times in your sanctuary where I have beheld your power and glory? Why do I just sit down in that dry weariness as if I don't know where to go? As if I have no hope? I have been to Your sanctuary so many times! I know how to get there. I enter your gates with Praise (Psalm 100:4). That is how I am brought immediately into Your presence and that presence changes everything. I am reminded that you are steadfast. You are fixed in place, immovable, not subject to change. You aren't going anywhere. It's me, I get spiritual amnesia! Because Your steadfast love is better than life, I will praise you. Remind me of all the times that I have looked on You in the sanctuary and seen Your power and let those remembrances refresh my soul. Remind me that that same power applies to all my tomorrows.

"Thou are coming to a King,
Large petitions with thee bring;
For His grace and power are such,
None can ever ask too much…"
John Newton

Your turn

Evening

Read Psalm 28. Commentaries aren't sure of the circumstances surrounding this Psalm, but I believe that it fits our circumstances any day. The scripture speaks for itself. "The Lord is my strength and my shield; in him my heart trusts and I am helped; my heart exults, and with my song I give thanks to him" (Psalm 28:7).

Read verse 9 one more time. David understood better than most what it meant to be carried by a shepherd. He could lift up his hands when he was helpless, and God would carry him. My prayer for us is that we will learn how to be carried, not just today, but into all our tomorrows. In surrender security is found.

You are our Almighty Father. Those words together are enough to thrill the heart because you are Almighty and yet our Father at the same time. Let it never stop being amazing to us. Thrill our hearts forever with the fact that You, the Almighty, hear our every prayer. Thank you that we need only lift our hands and You are there to carry us as a shepherd.

Your turn

Afterward and Challenge

God has been so good to me through this study. Truly these words were for *my* heart. God has used them to pierce me. And in His grace He has taught me that I should not put on mascara until I am done writing for the day! So many tears of refinement and joy have gone into this! In my daily life I continue to work out these truths. And that is exactly what I want you to do. You have begun a habit of reading scripture and having it become part of your prayer. Just because this book is over doesn't mean that habit should be. You have your Bible and that is all you need. Every lesson worth learning and prayer worth praying is between its pages. I beg you not to stop this new discipline of documenting your prayers. It will be the difference in your life. It will define your walk. I challenge you to, "Continue steadfastly in prayer, being watchful in it with thanksgiving" (Colossians 4:2).

Study Guide

Group Session 1

What made David's whole heart rely on a steadfast God?

"A car is made to run on petrol, and it would not run properly on anything else. Now God designed the human machine to run on Himself, He Himself is the fuel our spirits were designed to burn, or the food our spirits were designed to feed on. <u>There is no other.</u> That is why it is no good asking God to make us happy in our own way without bothering about religion. God cannot give us happiness and peace apart from Himself, because it is not there. There is no such thing." C.S. Lewis, *Mere Christianity*

God is our_____; there is no other. His spirit fuels ours so the more we are in contact with His the better ours runs.

David spent his whole heart on God, and in turn, God made his heart whole. What is a part of your heart you have denied God access to? Is there a part you are willing to let Him into so that He can make it whole?

Time is essential to your relationship with God. Even though God exists outside of time He created us within its parameters. The more time we spend on God the more we push those parameters towards eternity. Our time becomes less spent and more saved.

Take a minute and discuss ways to make more time with God even just this week. Hold each other accountable through the week to implement your plan. Here are some ideas:

·Stop to actually pray at lunch.
·Pray for someone else each time you pick up your cellphone.

Write your ideas here:

Time with God changes our reality because it reminds us of what is actually real. It narrows our focus so that we can see past earth into eternity. Where are some areas you could use a refocusing on eternity?

Group Session 2

How many times does the phrase "But God" appear in scripture? What reason do you think God had for it to appear so much?

As a group read the following verse and chapter aloud. This story is a great example of praise used to still the enemy.

2 Chronicles 17:3
Jehoshaphat walked in the ways of his father _____.

Read 2 Chronicles 20

1. They sought the Lord with their _____ on Hm. (v.3&12)

2. They knew the battles was the _____ to fight. (v.15)

3. Their only action was _____ for His steadfast love. (v.21)

Our battles are not usually as tangible as this, but the same tactical weapons are available for everyday use! The way to battle the father of lies is to praise the Truth. Our battles often lie in the mind. There is a reason that 2 Corinthians 10:5 says take every thought captive. Captives are taken in war. Satan wants our thoughts as captives. We have been given the weapons to fight back, but we have to choose to engage in the battle.

What are some practical ways to take your thoughts captive?

In Day 2 of this week we talked about this quote by David Martyn Lloyd, "Have you realized that most of your unhappiness in life is due to the fact that you are listening to yourself instead of talking to yourself?"

Talk about this quote and what it means. What are some ways we should talk to ourselves instead of listening to ourselves?

This week you were to write down some of your favorite praise lyrics. Take time to share them now.

Group Session 3 Identity

Take turns sharing your song lyrics from this last week.

We learned that _____ stills the enemy, but I want more! I want to be that arrow God uses to strike right to the heart of Satan.

We are identified in _____, He is our identity. Take some time to read the following Scriptures and be reminded of your real identity.

Romans 8:15-17
Hebrews 3:6b
Hebrews 6:18&19
Galatians 3:29

When Satan attacks our identity, who is Satan actually attacking?

We will act like who we believe we are. Our identity is based on our

_____and _____ of who we are. (Introduction)

These two faucets of our identity depend on one another. If our conception of who we are in Christ is off, then our expression of Christ is also off. Satan wants to ruin our conception so that we become ineffective. If he can get us to believe we are less than God says we are, it affects our expression of Christ to the world.

This week I want you to individually identify an area or several where Satan is feeding you a lie about who you really are. Write the lie on one side of an index card. Then, find the truth, in scripture, that refutes this lie and write it on the other side of the index card. If you are comfortable doing so, please share these with your group next week so that you can prayerfully support each other as you stand against the schemes of the devil.

Group Session 4 Sin

Sin at its core is _____!

Have someone in the group read these scriptures aloud. Look for similarities.

Hebrews 3:12-14

James 1:12-16

What do both scriptures warn against?

How do we guard against this deception?

Now read Romans 12:9 aloud for an answer.

Write the two steps below:

   1.

   2.

If we aren't engaged in a battle against sin, we can be sure that sin is still advancing. David put down his sword and paid dearly for it. This was out of character for David, and the lesson we should learn from that is that we are all capable of more than we imagine. Let that knowledge keep you vigilant.

I have always been fascinated by David's courage and the stories of his mighty men. They accomplished mighty feats and followed David loyally. There is a verse I love in 2 Samuel 23. It speaks of one of David's mighty men in battle who was so focused and driven during the battle, he fought for so long that his sword stuck to his hand. He literally couldn't put it down. "He rose and struck down the philistines until his hand was weary, and his hand *clung* to the sword." (2 Samuel 23:10). That word clung is the Hebrew word "dabaq" which means to join together or hold fast. The first time I read this verse, I thought to myself, "That's it! That is how I am going out, with my hand frozen to my Bible." I want to wield it so well that it is an extension of me.

Our victory is dependant on how we cling to our_____!

Are you currently doing battle?

What are ways that our "sword" can be used to battle sin?

Are there any areas of your life that you need to allow God full access to?

Now that we have discussed how sin is also linked to deception, share your index cards containing Satan's lie and God's truth about your identity. Are there any links in your life between Satan's lies about your identity and sin that you have struggled with?

Group Session 5

Read the following verses aloud in your group and then answer the questions together.

According to Psalm 3:5&6 David had no fear of what?

According to Psalm 5:7&8 David feared only whom?

Discuss how fear finds its roots in insecurity.

The favor of man is fleeting while the favor of God is forever. The fact that God's favor is forever does not mean that we will not face difficult circumstances, rather it assures that we will. The fact that God doesn't change demands a change in us. The problem isn't what God allows but what we won't let go of.

Discuss the aspects of God that are unchanging and what kind of change that facilitates in us.

If we are honest, we often don't fear what He might do to us, but what He might do in us.

In this space provided, list some of the changes you feel God would like you to make.

A.W. Tozer states, "Outside the will of God, there's nothing I want. Inside the will of God, there's nothing I fear". My heart has clung to this quote, and I have prayed that it would become more and more true of me. Living without fear frees you from bondage and makes you so much more fit to be used for heavenly purposes.

What might being set free from fear in an area of your life look like. What changes could it bring?

In the introduction to this week I said that the solution to fear was to, "Set his steadfast love before your eyes, then walk on in His faithfulness" (Psalm 26:3).

Discuss and record practical ways you can look at a fear you have and practice setting your eyes on steadfast love, and then walk into action in His faithfulness.

Group Session 6

Chose someone to read Psalm 109:26&27 aloud to the group. Who did David recognize as the person that had "done it"?

David was referring to his circumstances at the time, but this can apply to any of our circumstances at any time. He realized that God was in charge of everything that happened to him. If it was allowed, God intended to use it. We need to pray for our hearts to recognize and submit to God's actions in our life and willingly participate.

As a group or privately, think on some hard circumstances in your life right now. Share with another person in the group and pray together for a willing spirit.

According to 1 Corinthians 2:7 (NEB) what is God's secret purpose for us?

The whole cannot be attained without each of the _____ parts. The small and daily is our destiny. It is how God gets us to full glory.

Our purpose on earth is to be made fit for_____.

Chose someone to read 1 Corinthians 13:9& 10 aloud.

In the here and now, we only have some of the pieces of the puzzle. But it is also a reality that when the perfect comes all of this, the partial, will pass away.

Take a moment and pray together that you will not get wrapped up in what you see as real, but that you will have eyes to see true reality and grasp our real destiny. Ask God to give you eyes to see how He is working in you this moment for eternity.

Study Guide Answers

Page 119 Prayer; Fuel

Page 121 David; eyes; Lord's; Praise

Page 123 praise; conception; expression

Page 124 deception; abhor what is evil; hold fast what is good; sword

Page 126 man; God

Page 128 His purpose is to bring us to full glory; smaller; heaven

Notes

Week 1 title page George MacDonald, *George MacDonald An Anthology,* edited by C.S. Lewis, copyright 1947 by MacMillan Publishing Company.

Week 1/Day 2 – Corrie ten Boom, *Tramp for the Lord.*

Week 1/Day 3 – A.W. Tozer, *The Pursuit of God.*

Week 2 title page Andrew Murray, *Teach Me to Pray,* copyright 1982, 2002 Bethany House Publishers.

Week2/Day2 – David Martyn Lloyd-Jones, *Spiritual Depression: It's Causes and Cure.*

Week 2/Day 3 – Charles Spurgeon, *Treasury of David,* Psalm 6.

Week 3 title page George MacDonald, *George MacDonald An Anthology,* edited by C.S. Lewis, copyright 1947 by MacMillan Publishing Company.

Week 4 title page George MacDonald, *George MacDonald An Anthology,* edited by C.S. Lewis, copyright 1947 by MacMillan Publishing Company.

Week4/Day1 – Jon Courson, *Jon Courson Application Commentary,*

Week4/Day4 – Geroge MacDonald, *George MacDonald An Anthology,* edited by C.S. Lewis, copyright 1947 by MacMillan Publishing Company.

Week 4/Evening 4 – Text: Elvina M. Hall, Tune: John T Grape, 1865, www.hymnary.org

Week 5 Intro/ Because He Lives, Bill and Gloria Gaither, copyright 1971 William J. Gaither, Inc. (Admin. y Gaither Copyright Management)

Week 5/Day 1 - Jon Courson, *Jon Courson Application Commentary*, copyright 2003, Thomas Nelson Publishing.

Week 5/Day 2 - Geroge MacDonald, *George MacDonald An Anthology*, edited by C.S. Lewis, copyright 1947 by MacMillan Publishing Company.

Study guide Group Session 1/ C.S. Lewis, *Mere Christianity*, copyright 1943, 1945, 1952 by Macmillan Publishing company, a division of Macmillan, Inc. Copyright renewed 1980 by Arthur Owen Barfield.

Week 6 title page D. L. Moody, www.jesus-is-savior.com

Week 6 Intro – C.S. Lewis, *God in the Dock* (Grand Rapids: Eerdmans, 1994), pg 52.

Week 6/Day 1 - George MacDonald, *George MacDonald An Anthology*, edited by C.S. Lewis, copyright 1947 by MacMillan Publishing Company.

Week 6/Day 2 - George MacDonald, *George MacDonald An Anthology*, edited by C.S. Lewis, copyright 1947 by MacMillan Publishing Company.

Week 6/Day 4 - Jon Courson, *Jon Courson Application Commentary*, copyright 2003, Thomas Nelson Publishing.

Biography

Lauren Mitchell is an author and teacher who spends most of her time chasing her three children and the rest of it chasing the heart of God. She has a passion for prayer and sharing her own struggles to help others learn God's steadfast love. She desires for her life, writing, and speaking to make others yearn for a closer walk with God.

Visit Lauren anytime at her website www.thingspondered.org

Acknowledgements

I want to thank my husband, Pete, who, as always, is my rock. I would additionally like to thank my Great Grandpa Schwerha whose belief in hard work and family helped to make this dream possible in ways he never saw…at least not from earth.